Small Spaces
Beautiful Kitchens

ROCKPORT

Small Spaces
Beautiful Kitchens

Tara McLellan

GLOUCESTER MASSACHUSETTS

ROCKPORT PUBLISHERS

First published in the United States of America by
Rockport Publishers, Inc.
33 Commercial Street
Gloucester, Massachusetts 01930-5089
Telephone: (978) 282-9590
Fax: (978) 283-2742
www.rockpub.com

Library of Congress Cataloging-in-Publication Data
McLellan, Tara.
    Small spaces, beautiful kitchens / Tara McLellan.
        p.   cm.
    ISBN 1-56496-956-8 (hardcover)
    1. Kitchens. 2. Interior decoration. I. Title.
    NK2117.K5 M35 2003
    747.7'97—dc21   2002014889

ISBN 1-56496-956-8

10 9 8 7 6 5 4 3 2 1

Design: Stoltze Design
Front Cover Image: Brian Vanden Brink/Sam Van Dam, Van Dam & Renner
    Architects
Back Cover Images: Snaidero Kitchens & Design (top);
    bulthaup (middle and bottom)
Floor Plans by Robert Leanna

Printed in China

Contents

Introduction

> *"There are no great things, only small things with great love. Happy are those."*
>
> – Mother Theresa

In today's fast-paced, ever-changing world, many of us find ourselves living in tighter and tighter spaces. Whether it's a modern city loft apartment, a single family suburban home, or retiree condominium on the beach front, our kitchens—our comfort zone, workspace, entertaining area, and family gathering space—are shrinking. This does not mean we have to give up all those elements of style, functionality, creativity, and comfort that we treasure in our kitchens. Small kitchens can still become family gathering spaces, entertaining areas, homework zones, quick snack centers for after work or school, as well as inspiration centers for a weekend gourmet.

In fact, small kitchens provide a homeowner with the unique opportunity to create an individual expression of their kitchen needs, from traditional family comfort to contemporary style to modern metropolitan chic. Small kitchens can in fact be more comfortable and efficient than larger-sized ones, with fewer surface areas to clean, and a smaller, more efficient workspace, saving steps from refrigerator to stove to sink. Small kitchens pack a lot of useful activities and focus them into zones, allowing the primary chef in the family to be more organized.

> *"We owe much to the fruitful meditation of our sages, but a sane view of life is, after all, elaborated mainly in the kitchen."*
>
> – Joseph Conrad

Planning, building, renovating, redecorating, or reorganizing a small kitchen calls for creativity and innovation. Effective small kitchens share the same basic three elements: carefully thought-out organization, clever storage solutions, and space-boosting color and design elements. But it's not just building materials and architectural design that make a small kitchen work. A good design should reflect the personality and character of the homeowner in color and lifestyle design. Here's your opportunity to make your small space whatever you want it to be. Don't limit yourself. Don't think of your small kitchen as a cramped eyesore. Think luxurious jewelry box, chic ship's galley, soaring skyscraper shelving, efficient Pullman car, or minimal modular. Utilize all the creative storage, organization, and design elements that have already been incorporated into efficient working kitchens and make them your own.

Left:
Although most kitchens are not this cramped, there are some important lessons to be learned: Keep all essentials on hand, be innovative, and keep a sense of humor when decorating, and organizing a small kitchen.

Small Spaces, Beautiful Kitchens will explore all the elements—from planning to painting, cabinets to countertops, seating to design styling—necessary to give the reader the best work plan to make their kitchen a small, but effective, comfortable, and stylish environment. It will provide ideas for kitchens of all lifestyles, from city single to growing family to retired emptynesters. It will provide detailed tips, plans, and personal know-how from the pros in every chapter to illustrate how real kitchens can work on a small scale.

"Always design a thing by considering it in its next larger context—a chair in a room, a room in a house, a house in an environment, an environment in a city plan."

— Eliel Saarinen

This is a workbook, plan book, and an idea book. This book will give readers the materials they need to make their kitchens work for them. This book will even work to inspire those whose kitchens are not size-challenged! Let's start planning....

Getting Started

"The dinosaur's eloquent lesson is that if some bigness is good, an overabundance of bigness is not necessarily better."

– Eric Johnston

The first step when planning a kitchen renovation, reorganization, or redecoration is to determine your needs and lifestyle, and the needs and lifestyles of the primary people who will be using your small kitchen space. Get out a sheet of paper and list all your culinary interests. Love baking? Write it down. Avid stir-fry chef? Write it down. Are you only in the kitchen for quick cooks, reheats, and meals on the go? Write that down too. Think about what items you'd like to store, from baking sheets and rolling pins to oversized woks, and what items you'd like to use and display. Remember, collections, from vintage wine bottles to antique cast iron pots to colorful and collectible fiesta ware, can not only be stored, but can act as a unique design element in your kitchen, highlighting your own personal style.

Now that you've got a basic list, rank it from most important to least important. This step will help you determine the focus of your kitchen and enable you to communicate your design and decorating needs to your family as well as to design professionals. An important step when planning a small kitchen is to determine the specialty or focus of your kitchen. Think of a small kitchen as an expert chef becoming a master in one area of cooking. As you read and prioritize your wish list, it will soon become apparent what you will need to focus on or specialize in when redesigning or reorganizing your kitchen.

An ultra-chic apartment dweller's worktable kitchen compresses all the elements into an efficient culinary corner.

Kitchen Questionnaire

Out with the Old

Storage

- Do your cabinets feature time- and space-saving accessories, such as pullout drawers, lazy Susans, and adjustable shelves?
- Are your cabinets in working order (hinges and drawers open easily)?
- Is the finish clean, in good shape, and up to date?
- Do you have sufficient cabinet storage space for all your essentials?

Countertop

- Is there enough counter space to complete work tasks that you perform most often?
- Is the countertop material easy to clean, undamaged, and in good shape?
- Are the countertop colors and patterns dated?

Mechanical

- Do you have sufficient natural and incandescent task and overall lighting?
- Are all light switches convenient and easy to reach?
- Do you have sufficient electrical outlets?
- Is plumbing in working order and up to date?
- Do you have a ventilation system?
- Has there been damage done to your kitchen by past leaks or fires?

Major Surfaces

- Is the flooring attractive and easy to clean?
- Is the flooring slip proof when wet?
- Is the flooring level?
- Is the wall covering up to date and easy to clean?

Appliances/Fixtures

- Is the sink in good condition and large enough to fit your needs?
- Is your sink conveniently located?
- Do you have a food waste disposal?
- Do you have a dishwasher?
- Do you have a microwave oven, and is it conveniently located?
- Is your refrigerator large enough and conveniently located?
- Does your cooktop/oven work and does it fit your needs?
- Is the cooktop/oven conveniently located?

Room Orientation

- Does your kitchen flow pleasantly from the rest of the house?
- Is there a dining/conversation area within the room?
- Does traffic through the kitchen cross the kitchen's main work triangle?

In with the New

Function

- Do I want a new kitchen or a simply a new design style?
- Who is the primary cook?
- How many other family members will be cooking?
- How many family members will be using the kitchen?
- How many people will the primary chef be cooking for on a daily basis?
- Will children and/or elderly family members be using the kitchen?
- Does anyone in your family have special needs?
- Is the primary cook tall or short?
- What type of cooking do you normally do?
- Will you be doing basic cooking or more elaborate meals?
- Will you be doing much baking?
- How often do you shop?
- Do you buy any items in bulk?

Style

- Can you incorporate old elements of your kitchen with new?
- Do you entertain frequently?
- Will you be eating within the kitchen?
- What is the overall style of your home?
- What are some current styles you have seen that you like?
- What do you like about friends' and family members' kitchens?
- What activities other than cooking will take place within the kitchen, such as computer work, kids' homework, entertaining, and so on?
- Are there any special storage considerations to take into account, such as personal collections or wine cabinets?

*Courtesy of the National Kitchen and Bath Association

Next, start your own clipping service. There are plenty of home design magazines with great ideas for kitchen plans, new appliances, cabinet and countertop materials, and color and fabric decor. Clip your favorites and start a binder or folder to keep everything together. Also include paint chips or colors, wallpaper and fabric samples, and tile and laminate samples. Visit local showrooms and walk the home improvement aisles of your local hardware store to get material, hardware, and paint inspiration. Take photographs or Polaroids of friends' kitchens or kitchen details that you like.

Creating this kind of file will not only spark your imagination but will provide a concrete portfolio of ideas to share with your contractor, architect, or designer—if you decide to use a professional. If you decide to make changes on your own, a file such as this will help you plan it all out and describe to subcontractors, family members, and friends what kind of changes you'd like to make.

Finally, and perhaps most importantly, establish a budget for the changes you can afford. According to the National Kitchen and Bath Association, a not-for-profit organization composed of the best of the best professionals in the kitchen and bath industry, the average cost of a new kitchen will range from $15,000 to $26,000 USD, including design, products, and installation. Although this is the average cost of a brand-new kitchen, be sure not to assume that just because you may have a small budget that changes must therefore also be small. *Small Spaces, Beautiful Kitchens* will show readers how to make changes large and small to make your kitchen more efficient as well as more beautiful for a wide range of budgets. Many of the recommendations made here are projects that homeowners can do themselves or that they can recruit a team of family and friends to help accomplish. Simple reorganizing, making color changes, adding light, and focusing cooking and storage spaces can transform a small kitchen from awkward to astounding.

If you do decide to hire a professional, carefully consider professionals in your area. Professionals have all the expert advice and sound solutions that you will need to get started. They will be able to incorporate your personal needs with your style and budget requirements. Be sure to bring along your personal style list and folder of clippings, as well as your personal estimated budget so that they may be able to create your price estimates and draw up an appropriate contract of work to be done.

This U-shaped kitchen is compact but fully organized with a careful eye to details. Warm, earthy cabinet and floor materials are juxtaposed with cool stainless steel counters, backsplash, and hardware for a sophisticated feel.

"In architecture as in all other operative arts, the end must direct the operation. The end is to build well. Well building has three conditions: Commodity, Firmness and Delight."

– Henry Watton

With a little planning, creativity, inspiration, and organization, your kitchen can be small, beautiful, and effective. Small kitchens will challenge you to think outside the box of a normal kitchen, but in the end can become a unique space that fits perfectly with your needs.

From the Kitchen of...
The National Kitchen and Bath Association

It's helpful to keep these measurements and ranges in mind when making large-scale renovations or when bringing in nontraditional work materials, such as an antique armoire for storage or an old butcher's block table for extra counter space.

- Small kitchens—approximately less than 150 square feet (14 m)—should allow for at least 144 inches (366 cm) of wall cabinets and 156 inches (396 cm) of base cabinets.
- Wall cabinets should be at least 12 inches (30 cm) deep and a minimum of 30 inches (76 cm) high and base cabinets at least 21 inches (53 cm) deep.
- Small kitchens should allow at least 132 inches (335 cm) of usable countertop space at a minimum of 16 inches (41 cm) deep.
- The work triangle, or the area between sink, cooktop, and refrigerator, should have no leg shorter than 4 feet (1.2 m) nor longer than 9 feet (2.7 m) and should not be intersected by work islands or peninsulas.
- No major traffic patterns should cross through the work triangle.
- Work aisles should be at least 42 inches to 48 inches (107 cm to 122 cm) wide.
- If the kitchen has only one sink, it should be located between or across from the cooking surface, preparation area, or refrigerator.
- All major appliances used for surface cooking should have a ventilation system, with a fan rated at 150-CFM minimum.
- Controls, handles, and door/drawer pulls should be operable with one hand, require only a minimal amount of strength for operation, and should not require tight grasping, pinching, or twisting of the wrist.
- Ground fault circuit interrupters (GFCI) should be specified for all outlets within the kitchen.

Summary—Assessing Your Needs

- Clip and save ideas and photos from home design and decorating magazines, tile and laminate samples, wallpaper samples and paint chips, and pictures of family members' and friends' kitchen ideas to inspire, as well as to convey your desires to your design professional should you decide to use one, or subcontractors and family and friend teams should you decide to do the work yourself.

- Visit showrooms and walk the aisles of the home improvement sections of your local hardware store to consider materials, colors, styles, patterns, and kitchen plans, and don't be afraid to ask the professionals on hand for advice and ideas.

- In order to determine the needs and lifestyle for your small kitchen, make a wish list and essentials list of everything you will want to feature, repair, and replace in your kitchen, and order it from most to least important.

- Focus the specialty of your kitchen and create a working design and organization plan around it.

- Research and interview design professionals in your area and gather estimates.

- Establish your working budget and determine what kind of renovation you can work toward.

- Decide which projects you will use a professional for and which projects, if any, you will want to do yourself.

- Get started and have fun!

Chapter One: Organizing Everything and the Kitchen Sink

"A cook, when I dine, seems to me a divine being, who from the depths of his kitchen rules the human race. One considers him as a minister of heaven, because his kitchen is a temple, in which his ovens are the altar."

– Desaugiers, nineteenth century French poet

The first element to consider when thinking about reorganizing or redesigning your kitchen is to determine the kitchen's traffic flow and to establish the kitchen or work triangle. The kitchen triangle is a good way to determine how efficiently your reorganized kitchen will work. Three points form the traditional kitchen triangle: the refrigerator, the stove, and the sink. When planning or moving your triangle, think about flow from these three points, as well as traffic into, around, and out of the kitchen. You will want to minimize the flow of traffic through the kitchen, saving as much space as possible for the work going on within the kitchen triangle. It is vital to prevent major traffic from flowing though your triangle in order to keep a kitchen working smoothly and safely. Let's take an up-close look at the three elements that will make up your triangle.

REFRIGERATOR

One of the largest and most important elements in a working kitchen is the refrigerator. It is important to remember that, although almost every kitchen should include a refrigerator, one size does not fit all. These days, there is a wide array of sizes, shapes, and colors to choose from, and it is important to select a size that fits your unique needs. In a small kitchen where space is at a premium, you may want to consider a smaller refrigerator. Many avid chefs prefer to shop several times a week to keep food on hand at its freshest. Choose the smallest size that will fit your needs to free up much needed counter, cabinet, and work space.

Shelving units double as storage in this kitchen nook.

A smaller refrigerator is a good way to not only save space but also add color and personality. For example, a nontraditional, 1950s-style, bubble-gum pink refrigerator recalls diner chic.

If you are a baker, a drawer model refrigerator offers quick and easy access to supplies while working with dough and confections. Skinny vertical and compact half size models work well for city apartment dwellers and can come in fun retro designs. Smaller-sized refrigerators will obviously not hold as much food, but can provide you with an opportunity to purchase smaller amounts of fresh food as needed. With all the many stylish compact models now available, take time to shop around and research carefully.

If your needs do demand a full-sized refrigerator, remember that you will be limiting storage for other accessories, appliances, and cabinet items. A side-by-side refrigerator uses less space and can provide more storage for pantry items than a traditional-style refrigerator. Professional, oversized models are not generally recommended, as they take up too much needed storage space and use up too much energy for the typical home kitchen.

Whatever refrigerator you choose, be sure to allow plenty of room for full-sized doors to swing open, as well as for landing areas for heavier food items or for setting bags of groceries before unloading. Many experts feel the placement of the refrigerator should be at the most accessible point of the work triangle, allowing family members coming into the kitchen access to it even when not engaged in kitchen cooking activities. You want to make sure that people coming into the kitchen for a cold can of soda from the refrigerator will not cross into the busy work zone, so take the whole picture into consideration.

COOKTOP AND OVEN

"In the childhood memories of every good cook, there's a large kitchen, a warm stove, a simmering pot, and a mom."

– Barbara Costikyan

The next element to consider is the cooking area. A typical cooktop and oven combination works best in a small kitchen and can help to centralize all main cooking activities in one place. Cooktops can become a cooking and design focal point, as there are many striking and versatile cooktops, ovens, and vent hoods in multiple sizes and configurations. A smaller-sized two- or four-burner stovetop works wonders for kitchens that will only be used for reheating and meals on the go, while multiple burners, and specialized units for steaming, woks, and grilling can offer all the options a gourmet chef could desire. In fact, a fully equipped stovetop can eliminate the need for additional small kitchen appliances, such as electric steamers, mini grills, rotisseries, and toaster ovens, freeing up additional storage and counter space. Choose a model that meets your budget and cooking needs.

A stove is perhaps the hardest kitchen appliance, but it can add the strongest visual impact. A compact model doesn't have to be bland; try choosing a smaller model with an emphasis on style.

The stove or cooktop should be placed at the remotest point of the kitchen triangle, and protected on both sides from traffic flow. Allow plenty of room for oven doors to open and provide a sturdy, stable, heat-proof landing area for removal of hot pans and dishes from the cooking area.

Shelves or cabinets above cooking areas may store packaged food items that are not affected by heat, such as dried goods, rice, or pasta. Keep a neat array in clear jars or containers for easy access. A shelf just above the cooktop is also a good area for storing all the accessories a chef will need for cooking, such as utensils, spices, trivets, and oven mitts, or even pot lids. A hanging or wall rack for pots and pans above or next to a cooktop is also a natural setup for the busy chef.

Kitchen Sink

The last element you will need to consider is the size and placement of the kitchen sink. Sinks, like the refrigerator and stove, now come in many sizes, shapes, depths, and capacities. Deeper sinks are an excellent way of hiding clutter if you plan on doing lots of entertaining, but it is best to avoid sinks that are overly deep to prevent back strain while washing dishes, platters, and glassware.

Build a work center that includes everything and the kitchen sink. Your sink area is the perfect prep space for chopping vegetables, draining pasta, or washing fruit. Choose a sink with specialized prep boards, strainers, or faucets, and get the maximum bang for your buck.

The kinds of foods you prepare most often can also affect which sink and faucet configuration will work best for you. If you cook pasta, soups, or dishes that require deep pots, you may want a deeper sink along with a taller faucet for washing and filling of pots. If you prepare lots of fresh vegetables, you may want to have a sink with a chopping board, allowing you more room for preparation and ease of washing. If your kitchen will only be used for minimal cooking, you may want to stick with a smaller model, or even opt for a bar model to minimize the counter space that is used.

An undermounted sink works best for chefs and busy cooks, allowing for maximum use of surrounding counters and easily keeping work areas clean, as scraps or dirt can be pushed directly into the sink instead of getting trapped in small cracks and crevices.

Faucets are also heavily used tools of the kitchen and can be an important investment in the long run. Spray and single-handled pullout options help with difficult cleanup, vegetable and food prep, and filling of larger pots. Single-handled, lever faucets are also a good option for busy hands, children, or people with trouble twisting traditional knobs. Gooseneck models are stylish and provide the easiest way to fill tall pots. Some models can even regulate exact water temperature and come equipped with elaborate filtering devices for water that is just right for all your needs. Visit showrooms near you to see and test out firsthand how sink and faucet combinations will work for you.

"A good kitchen should be sufficiently remote from the principal apartment of the house, that the members, visitors, or guests of the family may not perceive the odour incident to cooking, or hear the noise of culinary operations."

– Mrs. Isabella, *Book of Household Management*, 1861

Small Kitchen Plans That Work

Now that we have covered the main elements that you will need to fit into your kitchen, let's examine the best working plans for a small kitchen setup. Although there are numerous kitchen configurations to choose from, there are three main kitchen plans that work best for a smaller space. As always, there are exceptions to the rule, so use these three layouts as merely a starting point when planning or reorganizing your kitchen. You can discuss further options with your architect if you choose to consider a more extensive renovation project.

The sink area is a good place to set up vegetable and fruit prep, glasses and beverage centers, as well as cleaning materials. With a little careful organization, the sink area can help lessen cooking and washing up time, and streamline your kitchen's effectiveness.

As if from the pages of a glossy magazine, this kitchen goes all out and takes on high fashion, modern look. The homeowners have decided to use their budget on high tech surfaces and appliances for an ultrasleek look.

GALLEY KITCHEN

The first small kitchen plan we are going to take a look at is the galley kitchen. The galley kitchen is composed of two parallel counter surfaces with a center aisle running the length of the kitchen. Establishing a good work triangle here requires two points to be on one side of the galley. Many architects, contractors, and chefs agree that the refrigerator and sink work best on one side of the galley with the stove on the opposite side and placed between the two.

Due to space constraints, seating is not an option inside the galley. An alternative is to set up a bar with seating outside the kitchen along one side of the galley, which is open into an opposing room or at the end of a run of cabinets. This can actually help keep a galley kitchen from seeming too closed in and opens up the kitchen so that a cook may converse with family and friends while working in the kitchen. It also provides extra eating and seating for everyday work, conversations, or special entertaining.

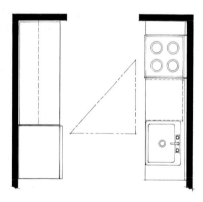

GALLEY KITCHEN

A galley kitchen is not only good for small apartments and dorm rooms. A small galley kitchen with an eye to streamlined detail can become a beautifully organized work center with graceful style.

THE L-SHAPED KITCHEN

With its wide open interior space, an L-shaped kitchen plan works best when you want to have multiple cooks in the kitchen, plan on inviting guests into the kitchen, or if you have a growing family that will need access to the kitchen while the primary chef is cooking. In an L-shaped kitchen, two work surfaces are arranged perpendicular to one another, comprising the two legs of the "L." Place the refrigerator at the end of either of the two legs, and center the sink and the stove on each leg for maximum efficiency with your work triangle. This plan uses corner space effectively, while leaving room for a wheeled butcher block, small worktable, or simple eating area in the center of the kitchen or at either end of the row of cabinets.

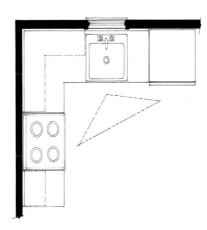

L-SHAPED KITCHEN

The L-shaped kitchen is a refreshing, open, and airy space that allows plenty of room for multiple cooks as well as entertaining, even when confined to a very tight space. Keep details light and bright to maintain a roomy feel.

THE U-SHAPED KITCHEN

The U-shaped kitchen wastes no space and is the most effective plan for a chef who wants to take charge and get cooking. Three counter surfaces form a U-shape, maximizing storage in all corners of the kitchen. The work triangle is easy to establish, with each of the three points placed opposite one another. The bottom of the U-shape will determine the kitchen's focus, whether it is a grand stove with all the amenities or a window with a view over a deep farmhouse sink. When you enter the kitchen, remember your focus and plan accordingly. While the open interior does leave some room for a work counter or table, it is important to remember that anything in the middle of the U will take away from the natural flow of traffic inside the work triangle, so keep additions and traffic in and out to a minimum.

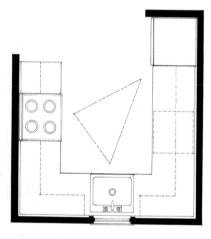

U-SHAPED KITCHEN

The U-shaped kitchen is perfect for the serious chef. The three countertops provide plenty of prep and storage space and the triangle is perfectly symmetrical.

From the Kitchen of...
David Page and Barbara Shinn,
Home Kitchen restaurant, New York City

Home Kitchen produces a gourmet menu from a kitchen space of only 75 square feet (7 m). Owners David Page and Barbara Shinn offer tips they've learned on the job about how to organize their kitchen and how to work when things really heat up.

What are your top five tips on organizing a busy small kitchen?
Here are our rules to make our busy Home Kitchen work.
1. Everything in the kitchen needs to be within one to two steps of each chef.
2. Our kitchen is organized so that cooks do not need to cross paths during service.
3. Preparations are simple and straightforward, with no more than three to four components on each plate.
4. Divide the work evenly between the kitchen crew so that no cook is overtasked.
5. Create clear and concise systems for communication between cooks and waiters.

What are some storage or organization solutions you've found work for your kitchen?
Plastic stackable one-quart containers fitted into rectangular ice bins. Sliding tray holders in reach inside the refrigerator allow complete use of space. Shelving high above the kitchen allows us to hide away large pots and pans when not in use.

What is important to consider when setting up and cooking in a small kitchen?
In our case, we considered the style of the menu we wish to present to our guests and built our kitchen around it. Try to be as versatile as possible. However, limit the cooking methods during service to two or three. This will allow the chefs to concentrate and execute these methods with a high level of skill.

How do you and your staff work together in such a small space during busy times?
It is either a ballet or a hockey game or sometimes a little of both. All kidding aside, when our staff is well trained, they perform like professionals. If the training systems were to slip, they perform like amateurs.

Working Stations

"If you can't stand the heat, get out of the kitchen."

– Harry S. Truman

Now that we have the basic components in place and the basic kitchen triangle established, the next step is to set up workstations and incorporate any additional appliances you will need or want to include. Be sure that any appliances you consider adding are essential. Smaller kitchens fill up fast.

Consider the work triangle you have established for your kitchen to eliminate work traffic problems when considering adding in extra appliances. Professional chefs set up stations for the three main activities of the kitchen: cooking, cleanup, and storage. Try to store all items where you will first use them; knives and chopping blocks should be near the refrigerator and vegetable prep area; omelet and sauté pans, along with whisks and wooden spoons, should be at hand near the cooktop; pasta pots are best kept near the sink for quick filling of water and draining.

Let's start workstation planning with the sink area. Standing in front of your sink, determine the most comfortable area for placing your dishwasher or dish draining area. Professionals suggest that this be no farther than 24 inches (61 cm), although this measurement is not etched in stone and can be customized for your space. Decide what works best for you, with what your kitchen has to offer. There are new dishwashers built especially for smaller spaces, so, again, do your research if you are planning on replacing or adding a new dishwasher into a small space.

Next, turn to the refrigerator. You may want to create an area around the refrigerator for groceries, as well as for food prep. It is a natural area for chopping, slicing and dicing, getting all items ready to be carried over to the cooking area. This is also a good area to work with pastry dough and confections that need to be chilled during preparation.

Finally, consider the stove area. You will want to store all materials, utensils, and spices that you will need close to your cooking area. You may want to have storage areas with wooden spoons, cooking utensils, spatulas, baking sheets, pots, pans, and spices on hand nearby.

If you are an avid baker, store all measuring cups, mixing bowls, and baking utensils in one area. You may want to have a special counter material such as marble for your counter surface material for this space. You will also want to keep mixers and blenders in large base cabinets within easy reach. There are many options available to help organize all of your needs, and these will be discussed in Chapter Two.

When hard at work in front of a stove, a chef needs to have all the equipment at the ready. The stove work center is the most important area of orginization. Items to keep on hand include extra pots, pans, lids, cooking utensils, as well as spices.

Safety First

From hot burners and steaming pans, boiling water and sizzling foods, wet surfaces and flame ups, the kitchen is full of accidents waiting to happen. In fact, most residential fires start in the kitchen. By following a few simple guidelines when designing your kitchen you can avoid common kitchen catastrophes.

- Use proper lighting. Bright task lighting that's focused on a work surface can greatly decrease your chance of injury while preparing a meal.

- Use slip-resistant flooring. Using materials on your floor, such as matte-finished wood or laminate, textured vinyl, or a soft-glazed ceramic tile will help prevet falls.

- Keep a fire extinguisher handy—ideally located near a room exit, away from cooking equipment and above the floor.

- Install smoke detectors outside kitchens and keep fresh batteries in them at all times.

- Keep electrical switches, plugs, and lighting fixtures away from water sources and wet hands.

- Consider appliances with lock-out options. Many of today's appliances are equipped with features so no one can use them when you're not in the room.

- Install faucets with anti-scald devices or buy pressure-balanced valves that equalize hot and cold water.

- Find a safe cooktop, one with staggered burners and controls along the side or in the front.

- Consider logistics. Smart placement of ovens and storage cabinets and rounded corners on counters will go a long way toward making your kitchen a safe place for your family.

"A common mistake people make when trying to design something completely foolproof is to underestimate the ingenuity of complete fools."

– Douglas Adams, "Mostly Harmless"

Small Appliances

MICROWAVE OVENS

When considering your cooking, reheating, and defrosting needs, you may want to take the opportunity to consider incorporating a microwave oven if you don't already own one, or switching out to a smaller, sleeker design if you already have one. Keeping a microwave close to the cooktop area can help out with major cooking tasks, such as reheating and defrosting. Smaller models, as well as under-the-cabinet models, can make microwaving tasks stylish and simple, while preserving vital counter space.

Microwaves can fit into corners, above ovens, or over refrigerators. Placing the microwave over a cooktop or range, which has become very popular over the past few years, is actually the least efficient space for a microwave, as you are more likely to spill or get burned trying to remove food items from a position higher up. If your current microwave is in this type of configuration, you may want to consider an alternative.

The best place for a microwave is on a platform on a countertop, which may take up valuable space, or mounted underneath a cabinet. This allows a more natural removal of food items and is easier for the elderly or for school-aged children to reach. Be sure to provide plenty of landing space for potentially hot dishes on the counter. Remember that adequate ventilation is a must for all heat-radiating appliances, so leave room above and below for plenty of circulation.

It is not recommended to replace stoves or ovens with microwave ovens completely, even in the smallest of kitchens, but as style, color, and size options grow, it is easier to find a model that will become a helpful tool in your small space.

While the microwave oven has proved its usefulness in a fast-paced world, other small appliances may not provide enough use to sacrifice cabinet and counter room in a small space. A small kitchen simply may not be able to properly store many small appliances such as blenders, toaster ovens, bread makers, mixers, juicers, and steamers.

LIMIT COUNTERTOP APPLIANCES

It is best when cooking in a small kitchen to streamline. Instead of buying an electric steamer, try investing in a high-quality steel or inexpensive bamboo steamer for the stovetop and stashing it along with pots and pans on a hanging rack. If you like to make smoothies and fresh juices, choose either a blender or juicer and specialize. Toaster ovens and toasters come in handy for making quick snacks and breakfasts. Opt for a toaster that can fit snugly mounted under a cabinet. Make your appliances multi-task! The hand mixer that does double-duty as a blender and the can opener that also works as a knife sharpener are valuable kitchen space-savers. The key word to remember when buying appliances or weeding out old ones? Edit, edit, edit.

ORGANIZED AREAS

Workstations can be a helpful way to keep your small kitchen organized. Try to think of every task as a small operation. Establish vegetable prep areas between your sink and stove with knives, chopping boards, and cleanup space. Create a hot beverage center next to the kettle or stove with glasses, mugs, spoons, tea, coffee, and sugar. Store baking supplies and work areas between the refrigerator and oven and provide mixing bowls, rolling pins, and baking accessories. Keep things at ready reach at all times and watch your kitchen and cooking efficiency grow.

Creating a specialized microwave nook not only frees up valuable counter space, it also provides an interesting cabinet detail. The microwave is an inexpensive and indispensible kitchen tool, and it's available in a variety of shapes, sizes, and colors. Choose a model that fits your kitchen's style as well as your workload.

From the Kitchen of...
Emanuel Loubier,
Dante's Kitchen, New Orleans, Louisiana

Chef Emanuel Loubier has seen his share of restaurant kitchens, but none as small, or intimate, shall we say, as the one at his latest restaurant, Dante's Kitchen. Not to be deterred, Chef E-man, as everyone calls him, and his staff have learned to work around and in their small kitchen and truly redefine the term *mise en place*, French for everything in its place.

What is the size and history of Dante's Kitchen?

When we first moved in about a year and a half ago, we found a kitchen, just that—a plain residential kitchen. In fact, the original four-burner stove was still in place. There had been another restaurant on the premises and they had built on to the rest of the house, but the kitchen had remained pretty much the same. I measured it out of curiosity and found it to come to approximately 230 square feet (21.4 sq.m).

How do you and your staff manage to work together in such tight quarters on a busy night?

We can have up to four people working in the kitchen at a time. That's a team consisting of two chefs, one pastry chef, and one dishwasher. Team is a word we use a lot around here. We all have to work as a team to make the kitchen a success. We've learned to divide the kitchen into stations for what we're working on that night and then dance around each other. We've gotten to know the inside and out of each others' personalities.

What are the storage solutions you've found work best for you and your busy kitchen?

Because we emphasize the freshness of our food, we've found that it works best to buy smaller quantities of everything. I shop several times a week for fresh produce, fish, poultry, you name it. We immediately transfer everything to clear plastic two- and three-quart containers and stack them up, ready to go.

Wire shelving is also a big help. We have wire shelving, as well as storage space, built into every available space, even over the doors. When you run out of floor space, the only way to go is up.

Lastly, we don't use a lot of extra or fancy equipment in here. We keep just the basics on hand to keep counters and work areas free of clutter. If it gets in the way, out it goes!

Summary—Making a Plan

- Determine your existing kitchen plan and consider which plan might work best for your kitchen needs.

- Discuss custom plans based on the galley, L-shaped, or U-shaped kitchens with an architect if considering a full renovation.

- Apply the kitchen triangle to your major appliances to establish efficient and safe traffic flow into, within, and out of your kitchen.

- Consider compact major appliances versus standard appliances to save room.

- Choose major and small appliances that fit in with your kitchen specialty. Give special consideration to a small microwave and its placement.

- Set up work zones like a professional chef for all your cooking tasks from healthy vegetable sink prep centers to elaborate baking centers to quick-cook microwave reheat centers.

- Free up as much counter space as possible by eliminating bulky appliances and accessories.

- Edit. Edit. Edit.

A high contrast marble counter and backsplash adds visual impact to an elegant small kitchen. The deep grain of the marble veins also mimics the pattern within the stained wooden cabinets.

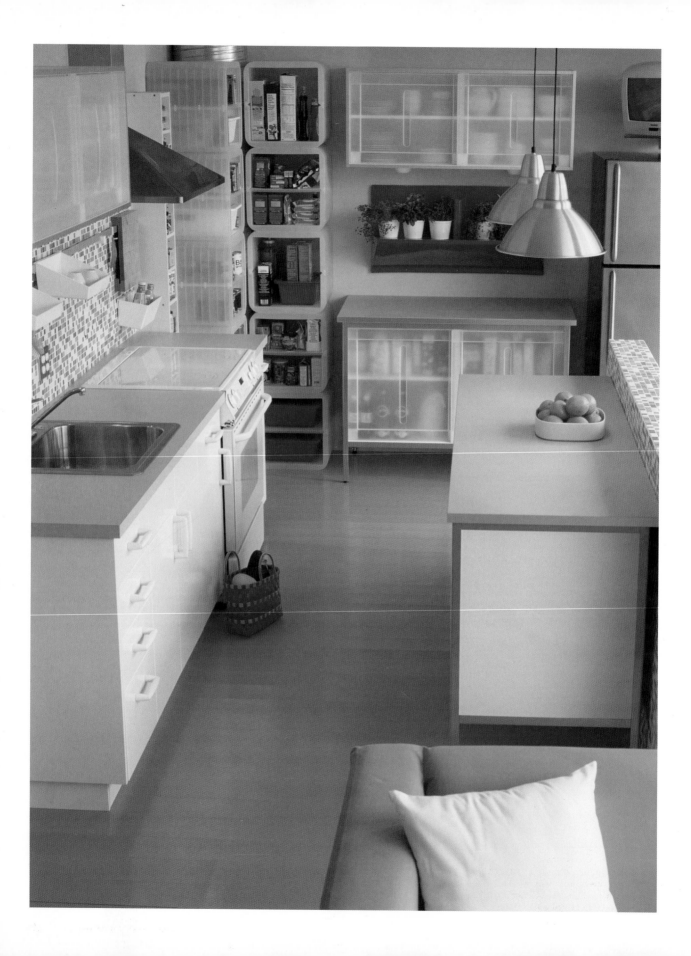

Chapter Two:
Storage—A Space Odyssey

Perhaps the most important element in a small kitchen, as in any small living space, is storage—lack of storage, effective storage, and hidden storage. In this chapter, we will take a look at storage solutions from the point of view of kitchen experts to find what works best for the kitchen plan you established in Chapter One.

"A messy kitchen is a happy kitchen, and this kitchen is delirious."

– Unknown

Getting Rid of Clutter

The first and most important step before renovating or reorganizing a kitchen is to get rid of clutter and to eliminate those things that are not often used. Do you find yourself making ice cream in your state-of-the-art ice cream maker only on the Fourth of July? Did your Aunt Mary give you a hot pink Elvis cookie jar for your wedding, while you prefer to have a minimal, sleek, and modern stainless steel kitchen? Are the thirty-five oversized martini glasses you received as a wedding present gathering layer after layer of dust in your cabinet? Don't store these items in a small kitchen space where storage is at a premium. Eliminate all of those things you do not use on a daily, weekly, or monthly basis. You will have to take a long, hard look at all of your kitchen items and be merciless. Throw away, donate, or have a garage sale of those things that are used less than once a year, that are broken, or that you simply do not like.

This colorful and eclectic studio apartment kitchen works because the resident has taken special pains to stay organized. Extras are kept off the work space and stashed in specialized storage areas. Clean, cleared counter surfaces help to keep a small area visually open.

Next create a closet or storage space outside the kitchen, such as an old unused armoire in your dining room, hall closet, or empty basement cabinet, for those items that you want to keep but that are used only a few times, or even only once, a year. You can also store specialty entertaining items, such as punch bowls and cups, family items with a special sentimental attachment, such as your grandmother's antique silver spoons, or seasonal items, like Valentine's heart-shaped cake pans or oversized Thanksgiving turkey platters, in this area.

Next, create a clutter zone, such as a plastic drawer bin, wire or woven baskets, or back-of-door organizers for small items that flow through your kitchen, such as pens, loose papers, receipts, mail, coupons, and newspapers, and make it a point to clean them out once a week. Clear your kitchen of clutter as much as possible. It will make renovating or redecorating easier when starting with a clean palette. You will probably need to schedule regular cleaning out sessions several times a year, as busy, small kitchens have a way of collecting clutter like a magnet. Now that you have cleaned away all the clutter, you are ready to create or reorganize the essentials—those things that are used daily, weekly, and monthly.

"Out of clutter, find simplicity. From discord, find harmony. In the middle of difficulty, lies opportunity."

– Albert Einstein

Going Vertical

One way to look at storage is to think of your kitchen as a tiny metropolis. When thinking of storage possibilities, think elegant skyscraper. Going vertical with storage is an effective and beautiful way to handle limited space. Floor-to-ceiling shelving eliminates wasted space between the top of cabinets and the ceiling, as well as dust-catching surfaces up high that can be difficult to keep clean. Make sure all shelves are adjustable to accommodate everything from your tallest pitcher to your pottery collection to your bulkiest small appliance.

Beautiful and strong woods, such as maple or oak, give the kitchen a traditional and elegant look. Flexible and light woods such as bamboo and pine are also popular alternatives that lend a clean, warm look. Sturdy industrial materials, such as stainless steel or aluminum, give a fresh, modern look. Add solid wood cabinet doors or frosted glass panels to hide areas that are prone to clutter, especially on larger base cabinets, and leave the rest open to give a relaxed and roomy feel.

The height of vertical shelving can work wonders to draw attention up and to trick the eye into thinking there is more space than there actually is in a room. One drawback is the inaccessibility of higher cabinets. Use this opportunity to invest in a beautiful ladder. Pair traditional wood cabinets with an antique, brass accented library ladder. Sleeker cabinets take on a loft-like modern look with a utilitarian Pullman's ladder. Contemporary modern looks can handle playful plastic stepladders in ultrabright colors such as lime green or canary yellow spaced along a wall of sleek white or platinum shelving. Be creative and use this vertical storage option to have a little fun with your storage. Do remember to keep only those things that you will not need immediate access to on upper shelves. Larger baking dishes, platters, and decorative objects are good items to place near the top. Add spotlights near the top of tall storage towers to accent items on higher shelves and to keep dark shadows away.

An L-shaped kitchen takes advantage of every inch of space, from floor to ceiling. Soft gray cabinets masquerade as elegant skyscrapers while cool blue glass accents add visual interest.

"Show me a man who lives alone and has a perpetually clean kitchen, and eight times out of nine, I'll show you a man with detestable spiritual qualities."

– Charles Bukowski

Open Horizons

Another flexible and beautiful storage option to consider is horizontal open shelving. Think clean, stretched-out vistas or vast, flat prairies. A clean line of open horizontal shelving creates a pleasing line for the eye throughout the entire length of the kitchen. This is a particularly good option for kitchens with low ceilings, as they distract the eye to the middle of the wall instead of focusing on height. Keeping the shelves open or using translucent glass front cabinets also works to distract from small spaces.

Open shelving is used in many professional kitchens, and for the same reasons they work professionally, so too can they work in a home kitchen. Open shelving keeps everything you will need to create a gourmet feast out in the open and at ready reach. If you are an off-the-cuff, fast-moving cook, things will be at your fingertips, from pantry items and spices to serving plates, pots and pans, and cutlery. Group items by size, placing larger items in the rear to keep shelves looking neat, and stack or nest where possible to maximize space. Be creative in your placement and stagger pots and pans or mixing bowls to create a visual pattern. Place brightly labeled spices and packages where they can be seen to add interest.

Professional kitchens also work hard to keep things organized and grouped together in workstations. These principals work well in a home kitchen as well. Keep glasses and beverage containers near the sink for easy washing and storage. Spices work well grouped near the main cooking area, as do dry goods, such as pasta and rice, magnetic strips for knives, containers for wooden spoons and spatulas, and bins for cutlery. Pantry items, baking materials, and vegetables store well in plastic, wire or wicker bins, over counter surfaces for chopping, mixing, and rolling. Make a kitchen plan, and stick to it, keeping your work spaces clutter free and efficient.

A double row of wire shelving over a sink not only keeps dishes and glassware at hand while cooking or after washing up, but also provides a unique, sleek storage solution that gives the kitchen a more open feel.

From the Kitchen of...
bulthaup kitchen architecture, Germany

Bulthaup has been creating sleek, beautiful kitchen systems with European design for years. But while the designers at bulthaup acknowledge that function is the priority in a working kitchen, they also know that the kitchen is also used as an entertainment and family center. We've asked top designer Chris Tosdevin for his advice on putting all the elements together.

What is bulthaup's philosophy in kitchen design?
Function and ergonomics are of foremost importance in all bulthaup kitchens. Bulthaup designers consider each family's individual lifestyle; the goal is ultimately a superbly reduced design. Lifestyle and reduced design; bulthaup is architecture for the kitchen, serving function with graceful proportions, clean lines, and honest materials.

What are the most important elements to consider when putting together a kitchen in a small space?
Educating a typical end user and customer that they probably use only approximately 50 percent of what they currently have stored in their kitchen cabinets.

What are the specific ways bulthaup has come up with to maximize storage and organization in a small space?
Creating a balance between storage, equipment, and workspace.

What kinds of questions should homeowners ask themselves when designing their small kitchen with bulthaup?
To open every cabinet and be very honest about analyzing what is really used daily, weekly, seasonally, and then prioritizing storage based on the frequency of equipment use.

What role does color and material play in bulthaup kitchen design, specifically with regard to the use of stainless steel materials?
Material type, i.e., stainless steel, plays an important role in hygiene and durability. The role of lighter colors can be used to create an impression of larger spaces.

How can a homeowner incorporate eating and entertaining into a smaller kitchen? Say in an open loft-style kitchen, how is that done effectively?
Part of our 'lifestyle' philosophy is to create open plan living spaces where living, cooking, and dining are enjoyed by friends and family in one 'great room.'

I don't like to say that my kitchen is a religious place, but I would say that if I were a voodoo priestess, I would conduct my rituals there."

– Pearl Bailey, Pearl's Kitchen

Solutions for Kitchen Accessories

Let's take a look at all the basic kitchen items you will need to store. We all have pots and pans, spices, pantry items, dishes, and glassware in abundance. Some chefs' hobbies also require storage of special kitchen accessories. An avid baker will need to allow plenty of room for the storage of large baking pans. A pasta chef may need room for deep pots and an area to work with pasta dough. Someone who entertains a lot may have more serving pieces and cocktail glasses than in a typical household. Where and how we store them is as unique as a chef's style, so, once again, you will need to tailor the basics to your own cooking and storage needs.

POTS AND PANS

Pots and pans are perhaps the most important tool in a kitchen, as well as the most used and difficult to store. Pots are bulky, pans are heavy, and in a small kitchen where there is very little room to move around and not many spaces for storage, planning storage for these items calls for you to be creative.

Some chefs feel so strongly about their pots and pans that they devote an entire wall to them. Julia Child's remarkable and famous kitchen is perhaps the most celebrated example of this kind of storage. In her kitchen, one entire wall is composed of old fashioned peg board, upon which she has added hooks for each one of her extensive collection of pots, pans, muffin tins, molds, and forms. A simple black marker outline of each one keeps things in their place as they are removed for use.

A traditional hanging pot rack is placed over a doorway and adjacent to a cooktop for a storage solution that is out of the way of the chef and hidden from the sitting room flanking the kitchen.

Although Julia Child's method is a bit extreme, specifically tailored to the needs of a world-renowned chef, and would not work for the tiniest of kitchens, there are some good lessons to be found here in her unique method. A peg board or metal grid is an inexpensive and easy way to store not only pots and pans, but also small buckets to hold cooking utensils or cutlery. If you have an unused empty wall or backsplash area, consider applying this method instead of leaving it empty. Hooks keep things in place and ready at reach. Peg boards and metal grids have other pluses as storage options: they are easy to keep clean, as there is no surface to gather dust; pots and pans are constantly in circulation, so they stay ready and clean; a wall of neatly organized pots and pans looks natural in place of artwork in a working kitchen. Consider it a three-dimensional kitchen collage.

Another easy way to keep bulky pots and pans at the ready and yet out of the way is a hanging rack. Racks can come in many different sizes, shapes, and materials, but the one element they all have in common is strength. Be sure to select materials that are likely to hold the approximate weight of all of your cooking pans combined. It is also important to consider the chain or connection from rack to ceiling or wall, as well as making sure the entire system is anchored securely, preferably from a support joist for maximum security. Keep in mind that sturdy does not have to mean bulky. Racks that are not as wide will keep overhead areas clear and can look sleeker in a small space, while wall racks work well with low ceilings to minimize clutter.

Baking pans and cookie sheets are also bulky yet important items that need special storage consideration. Many chefs choose to create special alcoves or nooks with vertical openings for baking sheets. A simple open cabinet box with a series of wood dowels or vertical dividers can create an area with a custom built look for flat pans and platters, baking liners, and other baking tools. Many areas too narrow for a full sized cabinet such as the space between a sink and stove or above a skinny refrigerator are perfect for vertical baking storage. Another option is to transform an old-fashioned, wall-mounted plate rack into a baking center for storing thin pans, silicone baking pads, and parchment paper. Cup hooks attached to the base make excellent places to store oven mitts or cookie cutters.

DISHES AND GLASSWARE

Dishes and glassware have many of the same storage needs as pots and pans. They can be bulky, are often fragile or heavy, and are used almost daily. When stored on open horizontal shelving, rows of glassware can mirror the clean lines of an elegant bar. Display collections of glasses in groups and by size, and backlight the shelves to add sparkle to a storage wall. Plates are also beautiful as well as utilitarian and can be racked front facing forward on shelves. Be sure to use rubber shelving mats on hard surfaces such as glass and aluminum to keep them from slipping and to reduce the risk of breakage and chipping.

Standard cabinets with solid wood or frosted glass doors offer other options when storing glasses and dishes; they hide clutter. For a mix-and-match collection, this can save a space from looking overwhelmed with too many patterns and colors. Try investing in organizing, removable and stacking shelves from the housewares store to double the amount of storage in standard cabinets. Keep only everyday dishes in these cabinets and relegate formal china, serving platters, and holiday items to a storage closet to maximize space.

In this well-organized kitchen space, clear glass cabinets display a neat collection of bowls and serving accessories. Clear plastic bins keep spices and pantry items bought in bulk and ready for use.

PANTRY ITEMS AND SPICES

Of course, the focus of any kitchen is food and spice, but what is the best way to store it in a small kitchen? It is best to think of a small kitchen as a fresh food specialist. While it is essential to keep a wide variety of spices and those staples every kitchen should have on hand at all times, try to limit the amount of food stored by shopping several times a week or just once, say a weekend visit to a farmer's market, for a few featured vegetables, meats, and side dishes. If the size of your family requires buying bulk food items, try storing larger bulk items in air-tight bins outside the main kitchen, in a storage closet, for example, and keep smaller amounts in sealed containers for everyday use within the kitchen. Refill as supplies run low from your secret stash.

Left:
Open, horizontal wire shelving displays glasses and plates. Bowls and platters are stacked to save space and to keep the look clean and organized.

Custom-fitted drawers house a collection of exotic spices, oils, and vinegars for a serious chef. Explore unique storage ideas with your cabinet specialist to come up with a storage plan that works for you.

Spices are essential to good cooking and are indeed quite easy to store. Some chefs only use the freshest herbs. This offers a unique opportunity to bring fresh green color and life into a kitchen. Try an outdoor or small indoor kitchen window box with all your most used herbs, such as basil, chives, or oregano. This will not only bring refreshing life and color into the room and offer the freshest of tastes within fingertip's reach, but will fill your kitchen with a natural and earthy aroma that will make it feel warmer.

If you do not have access to a kitchen window but still want to use fresh herbs, try buying them fresh in small quantities, gathering them up in bunches and hanging them to dry naturally along an "herbal clothes line." This can be a simple cord stretched from hook to hook with the herbs clothespinned as necessary, or you can invest in a drying rack from a floral supply shop. Find what works best for your needs, kitchen space, and budget.

Although fresh herbs are most desired by serious chefs, there are still some dried herbs and essentials you will need to have on hand. It is best to keep salt, pepper, curries, paprika, and the rest of your dried herbs near your cooking source. Try a simple photo ledge or plank-style shelf mounted to the wall above your stove, a hanging rack along a suspended shelf, or a stacking lazy Susan next to the stove on the countertop. Scout out home supply shops for the rack that will fit your space and your spice needs. You will enjoy having all your spices ready at hand when you begin the cooking process, so this is not a throwaway investment.

Food staples are a must. Walk-in pantry closets are a dream to any chef, as a pantry offers all the space one needs to cook anything. Unfortunately, in a small kitchen, the pantry is sometimes the first storage unit to go. On the up side, there are now many clever add-ons and options for storing all the necessities. Pantry closets can fit into cramped corners, pull out of a tight space, and spin out to take advantage of every inch. Sliding, pullout pantries take their cue from tight ships' quarters and RVs. They fit vertically and pull out to reveal a deep and handy space next to a stove, refrigerator, or sink. These are, perhaps, the best option for a growing family with lots of food items to store.

A small family, city single, bachelor, or chic senior apartment dweller might want to consider keeping pantry items exposed on an open horizontal shelf. Spices may be mixed in as well. Packages of paprika, cereal boxes, brightly colored tins of tomatoes, soup cans, and the like can become pieces of pop art in the kitchen, as well as keeping those items readily available and easy to find. Group items together by necessity and size, spices with spices, flour and baking powder paired up, cans of soup and vegetables stacked up no deeper than two to keep things at ready reach. Controlled clutter can be beautiful. Interesting labels become artwork.

"Dining is and always was a great artistic opportunity."

– Frank Lloyd Wright

COLLECTIONS

When putting together and establishing the storage needs of your kitchen consider those specialty items you will want to store or display. If you are an avid collector of fine wines or decorative dishes, you will need to keep these special considerations in mind. Dish collectors may want to store items in a way that will bring their collections into the decor of the kitchen and yet keep them at hand for use. Wine connoisseurs can now choose from a wide variety of cooling refrigerators in smaller sizes. Another option is to display a large wine collection in a space outside the kitchen, such as in a dining room or in a special wine room in a basement. In Chapter Three you'll find an in-depth discussion of storing and displaying collections in your small kitchen. It is possible to store and display in an effective manner.

A colorful collection of fiesta ware and vintage items from the 1950s is displayed on simple open shelving while every inch of storage space is used. Especially colorful or interesting dishes can be displayed hanging on the wall instead of a traditional piece of artwork.

A Perfectly Planned Pantry

A well-stocked pantry is a must in any chef's kitchen. Unfortunately, in a smaller kitchen, pantry space is at a premium. Following is a pared-down list of pantry items, as well as essential tools and accessories that every kitchen must include. Use this as a checklist when cleaning out an old kitchen or moving into a new or newly renovated kitchen.

Pantry Basics

- Aluminum foil
- Baking powder
- Baking soda
- Beef stock
- Beans, canned or dried
- Brown sugar
- Chicken stock
- Chocolate, baking squares and semisweet chips
- Cornmeal
- Cornstarch
- Cooking spray
- Flour, all purpose
- Honey
- Jams
- Ketchup
- Maple syrup
- Mustard
- Noodles/pasta
- Nutmeg
- Nuts
- Oats
- Oils, vegetable and extra virgin olive oil
- Peanut butter
- Pepper or peppercorns
- Plastic wrap
- Raisins, or other dried fruit
- Rice, brown and white
- Salt
- Spaghetti sauce
- Spices: basil, bay leaves, herbes de Provence, Tabasco, curry, chili powder, cinnamon
- Sugar, granulated
- Tomatoes, canned
- Tuna, canned or pouch
- Vanilla extract
- Vinegars, apple cider and balsamic
- Worcestershire sauce
- Yeast, active dry

Utensil and Accessory Essentials

- 1 large (10 inch to 12 inch [25 cm to 30 cm]) nonstick skillet
- 1 large (10 inch to 12 inch [25 cm to 30 cm]) cast-iron skillet
- 1 large (10 quart [9 l]) pot with lid
- 3 saucepans of varying size with lids
- 1 large roasting pan
- 2 cookie sheets
- 1 9 inch by 13 inch (23 cm by 33 cm) baking pan
- 3 mixing bowls of varying sizes
- 1 steamer insert
- 1 long-handled soup ladle
- 1 metal spatula
- 1 rubber or plastic spatula
- 2 whisks
- 2 sets of measuring cups, one for liquids, one for dry
- 3 to 4 long-handled wooden spoons
- 3 cutting boards, one for meats and poultry, one for vegetables, and one for fruit
- 1 chef's knife
- 1 carving knife
- 1 paring knife
- 1 serrated bread knife
- 1 serrated slicer
- 1 set steak knives

Miscellaneous Essentials

- Can opener
- Colander
- Pepper grinder
- Thermometer
- Timer
- Corkscrew
- Cooling rack
- Square grater
- Vegetable peeler

A super-specialized baking and cooking center has been set up next to the cooking area. Deep drawers hold rolling pins, cookie cutters, and pie wheels, while cabinet doors hide vertical storage for pans, platters, and cookie sheets, as well as a pull-out drawer for stacking deep bowls. A wall-mounted pot rack keeps sauce pans within easy reach.

From the Kitchen of...
George Monos,
Detailed Renovations, New York City

During his ten years working as a kitchen and bath contractor in New York City, George Monos has seen it all—from tiny kitchens to extensive bathrooms, and he has carefully guided clients though all stages of renovation and construction.

What is your advice to homeowners reevaluating their kitchen storage?
Take a good inventory; what do you use, how often and when. Get rid of excess.

What questions do you ask homeowners when evaluating their needs?
It differs from client to client, but some that apply to most everyone are:
- Do you cook? What and how? Different meals require different appliances, cookware, utensils, and food (which also store differently).
- Who uses the kitchen? How many people at once? Doing what?
- Do you entertain? How often and how many? Will you need hot and cold platters, staging areas, serving staff?
- Do you shop regularly? Fresh, frozen, or dry?
- Is there anything you want displayed or hidden?

What are some overlooked or hidden areas that offer good storage?
Storage gadgets, pullouts, lift-ups, etc., generally don't work. Keep it simple. Organizers, such as spice drawers, adjustable partitions, hooks, recycling bins, work the best.

What is the best do-it-yourself tip for homeowners looking to maximize space?
Get as many wire racks and plastic storage caddies as possible for clutter, bags, pot lids, cleaning supplies, etc., and use them.

Can you give one last tip to maximize the efficiency of a small kitchen?
If budget permits, the best way to maximize a limited space is to eliminate over-sized appliances. Most clients do not realize how much of their existing kitchen is occupied by appliances that are not used or needed.

A black and white U-shaped kitchen is simply decorated but highly organized with open and traditional cabinets. A uniform color and a cool materials palette keep the space open and airy. Pots and pans are kept directly above the cook space, while the homeowner's collection of glass and dishware is displayed behind elegant glass fronted cabinets. Clutter is kept hidden behind closed cabinet doors.

Summary—Getting Creative with Storage

- Sell or recycle items that are broken or unwanted.

- Store only those items that are used at least once a month.

- Store seasonal, bulky, or less often used items and appliances in specially designated areas, such as a closet, armoire, or basement cabinet, outside the kitchen.

- Decide which style of cabinet storage works for your kitchen needs, go vertical, or try open horizontal.

- Consider a combination of vertical and horizontal, open and standard cabinets, to accommodate your personal needs.

- Stay organized, minimize clutter and extras, and group items in work stations to maintain an efficient and effective kitchen.

- Store pots and pans in easy-to-reach, out-of-the-way areas, such as a grid or a rack, allowing more storage room for pantry items and dishware.

- Store spices near cooking or food prep areas for quick access.

- Provide as many specialty storage aides, such as vertical pan dividers, silverware dividers, pot lid racks, slide out shelves, lazy Susans for corner storage, and spice racks, as possible.

- Consider using pantry items, dishes, and glassware as decorative art on open shelving.

- Streamline your kitchen, keeping only essentials, and shopping several times a week to eliminate extras.

Chapter Three:
Decorating to Trick the Eye

"When baking, follow directions. When cooking, go by your own taste."

– Laiko Bahrs

You have organized your kitchen into work areas and created storage solutions that work best for your kitchen's activities. Now comes the fun part—decorating. Decorating is the best, and sometimes the cheapest and easiest, way to add the illusion of space in a small area. Start by determining the skill level you want to achieve in your kitchen, whether it's weekend gourmet to dedicated culinary chemist, and apply it to your budget. Next, match quality and price with the look you want to achieve.

It is best to select an overall warm, cool, or colorful palette of materials, from cabinets to paint colors, and use it to make your choices. The palette you select should match the feel of your home and match your personality. It should make you feel good, so play around with mixing and matching colors, materials, and patterns. Use the wish file you created of swatches and magazine photos to piece things together carefully. Invest in inexpensive graph paper and play around with layouts. Paste color, fabric, and wallpaper palettes on paper to see how different combinations work together. Although the design combinations are endless, there are three essential palettes we will look at to help you construct when decorating a smaller kitchen: basic building materials; lighting sources; and color application and pattern.

By incorporating luminous metallic tiles and earthy, mottled flooring, this warm kitchen becomes a calming Zen retreat. Bright but softly diffused lighting bounces off the stainless counters and metallic tiles. This elegant mix of earthy and metallic keeps this small space from feeling cramped and dark.

Basic Materials

When constructing or renovating a small kitchen, your basic kitchen palette will come from the materials you choose for the most important and useful elements, your cabinets, countertops, and flooring. You will need to determine what palette works best for the mood you'd like to create and construct around that, taking into consideration quality and cost. Some palettes to consider for small spaces are warm and cozy, cool and light, or bright and colorful. Choose the palette that works with you or your family's personalities as well as the overall decor of your home. Consider the decor in rooms surrounding your kitchen. Or perhaps you'd like your new kitchen to be a total departure from the rest of your home. From Zen tranquil, to urban lively, traditional home, sleek modern, or family fun, it is important to stick with what makes you and your family feel good.

CABINETS

Cabinets will dominate the kitchen space, so it is essential to choose a style that you like as well as a material that does not overwhelm the room. Cabinets will also dominate your budget, accounting for almost half of your total budget. Prices are based on the type of wood or other material, such as composite or stainless steel, they are made of, and whether they are ready-made or custom. Stained wood is forgiving and attractive, but you do run the risk of having cabinets that are dated after a few years. Painted cabinets can bring personality and life to a larger surface of your kitchen and can change with the times. Decide which works best for your overall color scheme.

Custom-made cabinets are designed and built to order for a specific customer. You will meet with a product representative or carpenter to discuss your needs and cabinets will be built to your exact size, shape, color, and style requests. Custom-built cabinets are handcrafted, and thus are more expensive than stock cabinets, but will allow a homeowner to fit a kitchen's needs exactly.

Stock cabinets are factory-made in a variety of materials. They come in a wide array of colors and sizes and allow a customer to pick and choose which units work best for their kitchen. Because these cabinets are mass produced, they may not have the same custom quality and durability, but they are much easier for a tight budget.

A cool pickling technique has been used on cabinets in this open galley kitchen to provide subtle color without hiding the natural beauty of the wood grain.

There are many kinds of woods that are suitable for cabinets. Each one is unique. Hardwoods come from deciduous trees, while softwoods come from evergreens. Hardwoods are preferable in areas where durability is a must, such as base cabinets and flooring.

Maple and oak are known for their strength and resistance to splintering. Mahogany is often used in fine furniture because of its beauty and stability. Cherry has a unique grain and rich patina that gets slighter darker with age. Hickory is a good option for its extraordinary grain and color variation, as well as its heavy-duty weight. Teak, redwood, and cedar are best known in outdoor furniture because of their durability and resistance to rot. Ash and hickory are excellent not only for cabinets but also for flooring, as they are both known for their shock absorbency.

Pine is the most popular of the softwoods, with its casual style and ability to take stains and paint well. It is also commonly known as the least expensive material, but while cost is important, it does come at a price. Pine is extremely soft, showing wear and tear, dents, and scratches, and provides a less stable base for hinges and heavy items.

There are many popular woods and styles to choose from when deciding on traditional wood cabinets. Visit a showroom to get a feel for how a large area of different wood cabinets will look. Remember to keep door styles simple in a small space to prevent a fussy feel.

Stainless steel and laminates are also great cabinet material alternatives. Both lend a more sleek, modern look than woods, and they are durable and easy to clean. Stainless steel surfaces do double duty, as they are not only attractive and durable, but also work well to reflect light throughout a small space. When using stainless on many surfaces, be sure to provide lots of indirect incandescent lighting. It is important to maintain stainless surfaces with specially-made stainless steel cleansing products to minimize abrasion and fingerprint stains.

Homeowners also now have the option of man-made wood alternatives, such as MDF, or medium density fiberboard. This material is extremely stable, sturdy, and solid. As well as being a less expensive option, MDF may be painted or applied with wood or other laminate materials, making it the most versatile option available for cabinets.

A sleek, ultramodern stainless steel kitchen is as useful and efficient as it is visually striking. Be sure to provide wooden chopping blocks for prep areas and use diffused task lighting indirectly to prevent glare.

Stock laminate-covered cabinets can be found in many ready-made styles. This is a good option for the do-it-yourselfer, as you are able to pick and choose units that will provide the kind of storage you desire without having units custom built. A design professional can help you put together a plan that will work best for your small kitchen.

After you have selected your cabinet material, there are a few handy tips to keep in mind when designing the overall look and utility. Glass fronted cabinets work best on an upper row of cabinets to create the illusion of open spaces, while standard doors on lower cabinets hide utensils, pots and pans, and clutter. Stick with a plain-fronted door without fussy molding and details to cut down on cleaning and dusting. Regardless of style or materials, cabinets are at their best when installed by a professional to ensure proper balance, fit, and stability.

Drawers are now designed to hold more than just silverware. Opt for drawers with special organizing features for utensils as well as spices, bottles, plates, and bowls. Consider installing a drawer with a cutting board insert for extra chopping space. Make sure drawers are fully extendable so you can reach all the way back into the drawer space, and made with sturdy locking features.

Since cabinets are the predominate budget feature in a kitchen, many homeowners opt to simply repaint existing dated, dirty, or overly dark cabinets a lighter color to open up a small space without spending a large amount of money. It is important to remember to use quality, durable paint that will last when choosing this option, as cabinets are the one element in a kitchen that will be used on a daily basis by chefs and other family members.

The rest of the basic building materials in the kitchen will also greatly affect the cost of your total kitchen renovation or construction, but the details are just as important as cabinets in making an impact on the entire feel of your small space.

Specialty drawers and cabinets can boost storage and work space in a small area. A faux drawer is perfect for chopping or resting hot pots, while a pull-out pantry allows maximum storage in a minimum amount of space.

Colorful laminates give this kitchen a fun and lively feel, are often less expensive than wood or steel, and can be combined for a unique pattern.

From the Kitchen of...
A modern take on Euro-kitchen design, Snaidero Italia, Italy

For more than fifty years, contemporary kitchen pioneer Snaidero has furnished luxury homes all over the world with exquisite Italian kitchens. From London to Las Vegas, Snaidero is recognized for impeccable quality, meticulous installations, committed customer service, and high style.

The design department at Snaidero has words of advice for the homeowner trying to create a small kitchen that encompasses multistorage and multifunction needs with style.

Can you summarize the essence of Snaidero design philosophy?

World-famous designers, stylists, and architects who have collaborated with Snaidero include Gae Aulenti, Giovanni Offredi, Angelo Mangiarotti, Paolo Pininfarina (Ferrari designer), Massimo Iosa Ghini, Roberto Lucci, and Paolo Orlandini. Snaidero brings together the ideas and disciplines of the past into the present and incorporates them with the ultimate advanced technology. Snaidero USA has worked with an extensive list of renowned architects and design professionals including Michael Graves, Luis Revuelta, and Julius Schulman.

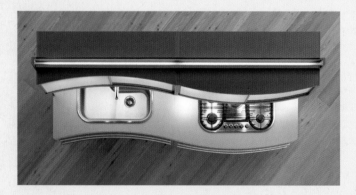

Can you mention some of the specific tools Snaidero has come up with to maximize storage and organization in a small space?

European kitchens tend to be much smaller than their American counterparts, so the utilization of space takes on greater importance. To meet this need, a Snaidero kitchen is, in many ways, designed from the inside out. The goal is to achieve maximum use of interiors without compromising the external aesthetics. The solution isn't more space but more utilization of space.

Snaidero offers many storage features with every model. For example, in the famous OLA model by Pininfarina, there is a large curved unit that may appear to be purely aesthetic. On the contrary, when you pull open the large drawer, you reveal a space to store pots and pans with a separate lid holder. This completely eliminates the search for the correct lid for your pot.

Snaidero also brings more functionality to the area under the sink. Instead of a cabinet, Snaidero uses a large pull-out drawer that houses cleaning products and/or separate waste units for sorting recyclables. The mechanism fits around the plumbing and eliminates having to crawl into your deep cabinet in search of the Pine-Sol.

The famous VIVA model by Pininfarina offers a complete martini bar inside one drawer. Also available are routed wooden utensil and knife drawers, adjustable can and bottle storage, adjustable dish, pot and pan storage, and built-in food-waste containers.

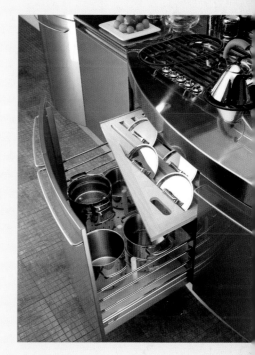

Can you tell us what role color plays in Snaidero kitchen design?

Snaidero offers the most comprehensive collection of colors of any European kitchen manufacturer. The Snaidero design team recognizes that people can let their individual personalities shine through in the kitchen as well as every other room of the home. For this reason, Snaidero offers colors such as Sherry Orange, Havana Green, Galaxy Blue, Desert Dusk, and Passion Red. People now look at their kitchens with the same regard as their cars—they want luxurious, well-designed cars *and* kitchens that reflect their personalities. For this reason, the Pininfarina collection's Dream Blue, Racing Red, Star White, and Silver Metallic are the most sought-after models.

What are the most important elements to consider when putting together a kitchen in a small space?

Elements like corner pull-out cabinets, tall pull-out pantries, smart storage devices, multifunctional cabinets, easy access to cooking utensils, pot and pan organizers are all some of the things Snaidero has taken into the Kitchen + Design motto. Also, they have some of the best kitchen designers in the nation on staff, with years of experience working with small spaces.

What kinds of questions should homeowners ask themselves when designing their small kitchen with a Snaidero representative or with their architect or contractor?

Snaidero is a Euro-style kitchen company with more than fifty years of experience in a market where space was hard to come by. Space-challenged kitchens are their specialty. They have adapted their experience in Europe with customers' needs in the United States, those who need to utilize the maximum storage in small amount of space. They offer the solution of a smaller depth cabinet with a mass variety of internal ingenious engineered accessories to fulfill the customer's needs.

How can a homeowner incorporate eating and entertaining into a smaller kitchen, for example, in an open-style loft kitchen. How is it done effectively?

One of our very newest designs comes to mind with this question. Sistema ES, by Lucci Orlandini Design, was designed completely with the family in mind—how to bring the family together into a common space. Also, the elements of Sistema ES—being completely freestanding and modular—are perfect for a smaller space.

One of the most concerning factors when designing the Sistema ES was to incorporate an island that was conducive to total family and entertainment involvement— meaning having an open-style feel for conversing as well as holding essential utensils, spices, knives, cutting blocks, and of course even a TV! Typical American family!

Flooring

There is now an outstanding variety of flooring materials available, from ceramic, leather, cork, or terra-cotta tile to bamboo, parquet, or hardwood flooring. It is possible to put a new floor directly over an existing floor, but this can also create problems. Be sure to check with a contractor or flooring representative to make sure all specifications for the material you choose are followed and fulfilled.

Let's take a look at a few of your material options. While durability and quality are important, it is also important to match your design needs, so be sure to keep your overall palette in mind.

Ceramic tile is a good option not only for counter and wall surfacing in a kitchen, but also works wonderfully as a colorful and rich-looking floor covering. Be sure to select a tile with a slight texture and avoid slick, high gloss options to minimize a slippery floor. Tile grout will show dirt, so choose tiles that are oversized to minimize the amount of grout line exposed. Another drawback is the rigidity of tile, so if you do decide to go with tile, be sure to provide plenty of thick, cushioned mats or rugs to prevent strain on the lower back when cooking or washing dishes.

Wood flooring is a beautiful, warm way to bring color and natural beauty into a kitchen. It is easy on the feet and back and has a natural "give" to it. Hardwoods work better than most softwoods, as they are less prone to scratching, denting, and splintering. It is important to remember to seal all wood floors in areas exposed to water, such as around kitchen sinks and refrigerators, to protect them from staining and spot damage.

Laminate flooring is a high tech, modern option with many pluses and few minuses. Laminate is a colored or decorative patterned paper bonded to high-density fiberboard and sealed with a plastic coating. With its moderate price, colorful pattern choices, and resistance to wear and tear, laminate flooring is a good option for busy families and chefs who plan on getting a lot of traffic use out of their kitchen floor.

Most new homes are built with the most practical flooring material already installed in their kitchens and baths—vinyl flooring. Vinyl flooring is still the most inexpensive, comfortable, and easy-to-care-for flooring material for high traffic, wet areas. It comes in limitless colors, textures, patterns, and combinations. Vinyl can be a good option for new construction, as well as for renovations of older spaces, but be sure to choose a high quality in larger sheets to eliminate seams, and install on a flat, smooth, and clean base to ensure long life.

Style counts. Run flooring in a pattern perpendicular to the cabinets to help make a small and narrow space appear wider, while keeping the color of the flooring similar in tone to the surroundings to maintain that open feel.

The homeowners in this kitchen used colored floor tiles in a bold geometric pattern to add visual interest to an otherwise solid white kitchen.

Countertops

Counters can also be created from a wide variety of materials. There are three main considerations when choosing your counter surface: clean-up, maintenance, and durability. Easy-to-clean surfaces are a must not only for chefs but busy families. Choose a counter that will stand up to your needs.

Do not be afraid to use a combination of materials where necessary and when budget allows. Stainless works wonderfully around a kitchen sink, while a special marble-topped baking center is a must for an avid baker. Tailor your choices to meet your specific needs.

Granite is a popular choice, as it is extremely durable as well as beautiful. Cool marble is also beautiful, available in many shades, and an excellent choice for avid bakers. Wood counters are a friendly, warm way of creating a traditional look. An island or work counter on casters is an excellent place for durable wood for chopping and food prep. Keep in mind the ease of cleaning natural surfaces. Textured surfaces, such as slate and granite, as well as tile, can be difficult to clean, but show less dirt, while smooth and lighter surfaces are easy to clean but show stains and show every speck of dirt.

Man-made materials, such as Corian or Formica, provide a wide array of color and texture options. Good quality laminates are the easiest choice for a tight budget, are extremely durable, as well as attractive, in almost any kitchen. Stainless steel is becoming a popular and striking choice for counter surfaces, as well as cabinets. Stainless steel is expensive but is unique in its look. Remember that stainless steel is easy to clean, but shows dirt easily, as well as smudges and fingerprints.

Light-colored wood countertops coordinates with the wooden base cabinets and provides visual contrast to the colorful tile backsplash.

A combination of tiles in earth tones is a good starting place when putting together a warm and organic palette.

A combination of tiles in earth tones is a good starting place when putting together a warm and organic palette.

Ceramic tiles are extremely heat resistant and come in many thicknesses and sizes for use not only on counters, but also on backsplashes, floors, and walls. Colorful tiles are a good way to create a variety of moods from an easy to a clean, traditional look with white subway tiles to a colorful modern mosaic-inspired work of art. Diagonal patterns work best to make a small space appear larger. Tiles come in many shapes, sizes, colors, and finishes, so it is best to find a local tile supplier and take a look at samples in person.

It is best to determine your budget first and then choose a tone and material palette that works best for you and your kitchen. Whether you choose traditional wood cabinets or stainless, tile, or Formica flooring, and granite or laminate countertops, there are a wide range of colors and patterns available. Using a mix of styles and colors can create the mood that is appropriate for your small space.

Warm and Organic Palette

Creating warmth in a small kitchen is an easy and organic way to bring in natural materials. Choosing woods with a rich but not dark tone, such as red oak or mahogany, will bring in earthy color without making the walls close in on a small kitchen. Traditional cabinets stacked floor to ceiling give the impression of an old-fashioned, elegant kitchen. Try pairing wood cabinets with handpainted tile or granite backsplash and counters. Nickel and gunmetal finished hardware continue the antique look without being brassy. Wood or natural cork tile flooring to match the cabinet color completes the look, for a kitchen look reminiscent of an old manor or an elegant sailing ship.

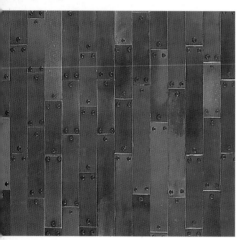

Warm woods, spicy colored walls and accessories, and a natural stone countertop create a warm and inviting space.

From the Kitchen of...
The Right Brothers, New Orleans, Louisiana

Custom contractor and cabinetmakers, Right Brothers in New Orleans, Louisiana, have specialized in renovations of old homes using traditional woods, such as oak and mahogany, but they also have experience working with such nontraditional materials like as cypress and cedar. They give us their tips on getting your kitchen cabinets right.

What kinds of woods or cabinet material would you recommend for a small kitchen?
It really depends on the light and the style of the rest of the home. Take a look at surrounding rooms and use the color and wood tones to match with them.

Why is it beneficial for a homeowner to use custom cabinets rather than stock?
Although the face frames and doors of many higher-end stock cabinets look great and are generally well constructed, most of the actual boxes are made of particle board or fiberboard and don't hold up well to prolonged use in well-used kitchens. This is true of the drawer boxes as well. Custom cabinet boxes are generally built of cabinet grade ¾ inch (2 cm) plywood with a veneer of the same wood or material used for the face frame, drawer faces, and doors. High-end custom drawer boxes are built of solid stock in the wood of choice and are constructed using dovetail joinery, which is far superior to and stronger than nails or screws.

Another advantage is that custom cabinets can be built to match the architectural details in the rest of the home and/or built to maximize the usable space in small or unique kitchens. No spacer units are used and symmetry can be maintained for a unified and pleasing design throughout the kitchen.

What is your advice to homeowners reevaluating their kitchen storage?

First and foremost, they should consider what kind of kitchen they want. Is it intended to be a gourmet's kitchen or a space for family and friends to socialize? Who will be using the kitchen, and who is the primary cook? What kinds of cooking will be done within the space?

The second thing to consider (especially in small kitchens) is what are the most used items and what items are just in the way most of the time? Don't be afraid to get rid of the Crock-Pot if all you ever use is a wok. And don't shy from putting grandma's finger bowls in storage until she comes to dinner. We also find that many small kitchens are in older houses or buildings that may not have a lot of square footage but do have high ceilings, extra tall or additional wall cabinets can be installed, and less used display items can be accessed with a step ladder.

What is the best do-it-yourself tip to homeowners looking to add efficiency and storage to their small kitchen?

Spring cleaning is essential to eliminate clutter and items that are not often used and organizing the kitchen to suit the way it is actually needed.

Cool and Light Palette

Bright white palettes remind us of cool spring afternoons, clean linens drying in the breeze, fresh air, and sunshine. Clean white or light-colored woods such as white oak or hickory, and a combination or open and glass-fronted shelving brings light into a small kitchen space. Complement shelving with a matte stainless steel backsplash or counter surface, which work well to reflect light. Clean and cool marble counters and backsplashes also work well and are as functional as they are beautiful. Chrome and nickel hardware continues with a sleek and cool theme. Flooring should remain light in color to reflect light up into a small space. Vinyl tile in a simple color and texture work best to coordinate with a lighter color palette to create a clean and open space.

 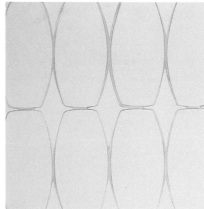

Icy blue-green painted cabinets are crisp and
cool and bring out the detail of the paneling.
A warm mahogany bar feature provides a shock
of contrast.

Rich wood floors provide a warm base for this kitchen, which mixes and matched colors and materials for a bright, colorful palette. Stained wood base cabinets are topped with cactus green and sunny yellow laminates. A mosaic tile backsplash adds texture and pattern, while a stainless steel cooktop reflects light. An earth-colored accent wall completes the look.

Bright and Colorful Palette

It is easy to express personality, warmth, and character in a kitchen with lots of color. Cabinets painted a uniform bright color blend together for a fun and lively look that bring a small kitchen to life. Canary yellow, ocean blue, and racy red look clean and uniform when used floor-to-ceiling in a small kitchen. Contrast with darker shades to add depth, such as rich cherry cabinets with multicolored tile backsplashes and counters, or match color for color for a more uniform look. Carry your theme through to your flooring with a lively linoleum or colorful tile. Or go organic with soft leather tile flooring that is warm and ever-changing. Bright and colorful palettes banish dreariness and allow a kitchen to have a little fun.

Exceptional Palette

Although many kitchen designs stick with the norm, there are some that venture outside to the extreme. These are small spaces with grand notions. These are small spaces that push the envelope. The message here is to be adventurous. Use exotic woods, such as teak or cypress, throughout an entire kitchen for a sophisticated cabin feel. Floor to ceiling chrome kitchens look sleek and modern and reflect lots of light for a luminous and cool feel. Towering black cubbyholes are the ultimate in elegant sophistication and are striking when paired with glittering tile walls and floors. Experiment until you find what works best for you.

Summary—Creating a Mood

- Determine your kitchen's needs, from professional to casual level, and your renovation or construction budget in order to choose materials that will work best for your cooking and lifestyle needs.

- Select a mood palette for your kitchen decor, from warm to cool to colorful, or a combination of many.

- Choose cabinets based on quality, color, and cost, and, while budget may be the biggest factor in making your decision, do not forgo your design needs completely. Choose something you will like and feel good about for years to come.

- Select flooring that is durable and nonslip to complement your cabinet and counter surfaces.

- Countertops should be able to stand up to every activity in your kitchen, while maintaining your design integrity. Collect samples of surfacing before making your final decision and consider maintenance as well as cost.

A harmonious palette is created by mixing and matching materials—a bold copper vent hood and bar base, stainless work counter, warm wood flooring, patterned laminate counters, and bold tile walls. Do not be afraid to use many different materials to create a look that works for you.

A warm, shining space is created for a couple looking for a kitchen that is efficient and organized, but that also has style. Stainless steel counters, cabinets, and accessories keep everything in its place, while warm wood floors and plenty of natural and incandescent lighting keep the space from being cold.

From the Kitchen of...
Douglas Teiger,
Abramson Teiger Architects, California

Architect Douglas Teiger has created a tiny, shining dream kitchen (left) for a sophisticated couple with a desire for a clean and well lit place.

What is the size of this seemingly large condo kitchen?
This kitchen is tiny. It measures 8 feet by 9 feet (2.4 m by 2.7 m). What's more impressive is the wonderful, oversized skylight, which measures 3 feet by 7 feet (0.9 m by 2.1 m), providing lots of light for this small space.

What did the clients tell you they were looking for when they approached you about their kitchen renovation?
This is a very sophisticated, empty-nest couple who are starting a new phase of their lives. They love to entertain and wanted a kitchen that would allow them to do just that. The wife is also a psychologist with a lifelong secret dream to become a surgeon. I came up with a kitchen that fills all of those needs. We've used bulthaup cabinets and accessories to keep everything in its place. The result is a very functional small space with the clean and organized feel of an operating room.

How did you keep this kitchen, which is almost entirely made up of stainless steel surfaces, from becoming cold?
Lighting, especially in a small space, is essential. Light is brought in not only from the skylight, but also from plenty of task lighting. It is important to diffuse lighting when working with stainless steel. You want light to be bounced around gently without creating glare.

What is the statement that you hoped would come across with this design?
This kitchen emphasizes organization, light, and verticality. The entrance to the kitchen is comprised of four equally sized planes, one of flamed granite, one open space, which is the entrance, one smooth plaster surface, and one of fire-etched glass. This emphasizes the verticality even before you enter the kitchen. Once in the kitchen, the skylight and the shining surfaces reflecting light throughout creating a warm environment for cooking up culinary delights.

Lighting

When working in a small space, especially a small kitchen space, lighting takes on a crucial role, not only in effectiveness but also warmth, style, and comfort. It is best to provide as much light as the room will allow, with adjustable incandescent spotlights whenever possible. Most older homes only provide a single light source in the middle of the ceiling. A single light source is not sufficient for any kitchen, regardless of size. A balance of both natural and incandescent light is best when possible, while clever use of incandescent light is essential when working with a space devoid of natural light.

Be sure to provide plenty of mirrored or reflective surfaces to allow light to bounce from corner to corner. Stainless steel or chrome hardware, metallic backsplashes and matte steel surfaces, decorative mirrors, glass fronted cabinets and glassware displays are all good ways to reflect light within a small space. Now let's take a look at light sources.

Well thought out task lighting under countertops makes cooking and food prep easy, while bringing warmth and eliminating shadows.

Natural Lighting

Natural light from windows or skylights is the most preferred way of letting warm, bright light into a smaller kitchen. Natural sunlight adds depth to a kitchen, keeps a small space from seeming closed in, and saves on the electricity bill. When constructing or renovating a kitchen, one easy rule to keep in mind when thinking about adding natural light is the 10 percent rule. For example, if your kitchen covers one hundred fifty square feet (13.9 sq. m), you should have at least 15 square feet (1.4 sq. m) of windows or skylights. A row of glass shelves displaying glassware, white earthenware or potted herb plants in front of a row of windows, not only provides more storage but also reflects light back into a room.

Skylights are also a good alternative addition to wall windows in small kitchens. Skylights open a small space vertically, creating not only the illusion of extra height but also bringing in light and color. A pale or brightly patterned floor can help to reflect light back up and into a room, so keep all materials in mind. You may want to consider retractable shades if you do live in a warm and sunny climate for those days that the sun warms up a kitchen a bit too much.

Minimize window treatments or eliminate them altogether to allow the maximum amount of natural to light to flood through. Valences, simple box cornices, or a lightly draped pole are a good way to frame a window with softly textured or patterned fabric without covering the main portion of a window. Cabinets can be built in an open casement style in front of a window and stacked with translucent glassware to provide extra storage and shine.

Open cabinets in front of a large casement window allow light to pass through a collection of glassware. Shining stainless steel countertops help reflect light back up into the room.

Incandescent Lighting

There are many ways to incorporate incandescent lighting into a small kitchen. A bright overhead light works to cast a warm yellow glow throughout the kitchen. Be sure to stick to a warmer incandescent bulb instead of fluorescent to keep things warm. Fluorescent lighting will give a cold, blue tone to a room and detracts from colors used to decorate a room. In recent years, halogen lighting has become the favorite lighting choice. Halogen lighting lends a whiter cast to a room than traditional incandescent lighting, allowing the room's true color and decor to pop.

In addition to overhead lighting, task lighting is an essential way to spread light into specific work areas. One good way to bring additional lighting into a small room is through the use of track lighting. These are small lights mounted on a flexible track that can flex and run in almost any shape along a kitchen ceiling. Lights are adjustable and can be fitted to illuminate every corner of your space. Track lighting has come a long way from the large mounted spotlights that were popular in the 1980s. Track lighting is now a striking alternative to traditional lighting sources.

Countertops are also often underilluminated. This problem can easily be solved by mounting low-voltage halogen lighting beneath cabinets. This allows the counter surface to become a well-lit workspace, making everyday cooking tasks easier and eliminating dim corners and shadowy cabinet overhang. Mount task lighting over counter spaces as close to the back wall as possible. This will eliminate glare and reflection from counter surfaces.

Track lighting is a useful and attractive way to bring incandescent lighting into a room. Track lighting can take the shape of any space and and lights are adjustable.

Recessed lights mounted along the perimeter of a kitchen create an even glow throughout an entire kitchen space. Recessed lights can be dimmed and adjusted for custom control. Professional lighting designers can help give you the right tools and ideas to bring recessed lighting into a kitchen area.

Cabinets can also be backlit, with the light shining through clear or frosted-glass fronts to accent collections of glass or pottery. Just as one would illuminate a display case of fine collectibles, everyday glassware can become a shining display when lit from within.

This kitchen/dining room combination makes good use of many different light sources. Focused recessed lighting, overhead lighting, and a decorative pendant light over the eating area all bring warm incandescent light to every corner of the room.

Summary—Designing with Light

- Do not settle for one light source, even in the smallest of kitchens. Provide at least three sources of light, if possible, one natural, and two incandescent.

- The more natural light, the better in a small kitchen. Windows should cover at least 10 percent of the total square footage of the room.

- Skylights are a good way to open up a small space vertically, while providing an extra source of light.

- Be sure to provide plenty of incandescent lighting, in addition to natural, to fully illuminate a kitchen at night.

- Choose warm incandescent lighting sources over fluorescent, which can wash out the color in a room and make the overall feeling too cold.

An impressive skylight and warm, white walls transform a tiny London apartment kitchen to a glowing galley space.

Color Boost

"When I'm old and gray, I want to have a house by the sea. And paint. With a lot of wonderful chums, good music, and booze around. And a damn good kitchen to cook in."

– Ava Gardner

The same palettes used in the materials section also work well when determining your paint color, wallpaper, fabric, and pattern schemes for your small kitchen. You may want to stick with only solid color painted walls or go with a more outstanding pattern in wallpaper, fabric, or mosaic tile. Whatever you choose, make sure it feels good to you and gives your kitchen the feeling you want.

There are many ways to bring color into a kitchen space. Try a backsplash with colorful handpainted tile or a custom stenciled design. Window treatments add soft folds of color and pattern. Multicolored throw rugs make a kitchen floor a better surface for work and walking. Tablecloths, placemats, and decorative plate settings will liven up a small kitchen table and invite guests into the space. Even the smallest hit of color adds accent with subtle effects and can transform a bland vanilla kitchen to an exciting, fun, and stimulating space. Dishtowels in cheerful vintage shades of canary yellow or ragtime red add a homey feel. Bring your appliances into the act and have a little fun. Coffeepots, toasters, blenders, and even chopping boards now come in every color of the rainbow, and since they will be sitting out on the counter every day, might as well give a little color boost to the room.

Painting a kitchen is an easy and relatively inexpensive way to cheer up a small space and really bring color into the room in a big way. But keep in mind, there are a few painting tips you should follow when decorating a small room. Try painting any molding or trim the same color as the wall to create a continuous, open feel. Painting opposite walls the same brighter accent color also helps to create a more open feel. Ceilings should be brighter or lighter than wall colors to allow the eye to travel up.

If you want to expand your kitchen to give it that wide open feel, try using cool, pale or understated colors and spread them out over large areas. If your desire is to create a tiny kitchen nook with a cozy feel, choose warm, dark shades or contrast many bright colors all throughout the room. Don't forget to consider the ceiling color when transforming a small room with paint. Warm, dark colors will make a ceiling appear to be lower, while pastel tints will make a ceiling lift up.

A tucked-away kitchen is boosted with bright aqua colored cabinets. The zigzag white trim along the stairs adds a visual boost, while shining white oversized tiles and perky white enamel hardware continue the cheerful feel.

Color Coded

When selecting the color palette that is right for your small space, keep in mind the following color associations to evoke the mood that fits with your lifestyle and design. Color can overwhelm, so be sure to take the negative associations into consideration. Sometimes too much color can be a bad thing!

	POSITIVE	NEGATIVE
RED	Excitement, energy, passion, heat, power	Danger, fire, aggression
YELLOW	Joy, happiness, sunshine, idealism	Hazard, illness, dishonesty
BLUE	Peace, tranquility, calm, harmony, trust	Cold, appetite suppressant
ORANGE	Energy, vitality, vibrancy, warmth	Flamboyant, demanding
GREEN	Nature, environment, healthy, good luck	Jealousy, envy
PURPLE	Spirituality, nobility, mysterious	Arrogance, mourning
GRAY	Security, reliability, intelligence, solid	Boring, sadness, old age
BROWN	Earthy, hearth, home, comfort, simplicity	Dirty, dull
WHITE	Purity, cleanliness, peacefulness, precision	Cold, sterile, clinical
BLACK	Sophistication, power, formality, wealth	Fear, death, anger

Color Questionnaire

When selecting a color palette for your kitchen, it's important to marry style with the personality of you and your family. Below are some simple questions to ask yourself in order to determine your personal color preferences.

- What is your favorite color?
- What is your least favorite color?
- Try taking a look at all shades of color, even ones you don't like. Peach can work beautifully in a small kitchen, even if you hate orange.
- What is the predominate color of surrounding rooms, and most important, the rooms directly adjacent to the kitchen?
- Do you gravitate to bright and bold colors or more subtle shades or pastels?
- Do you prefer neutrals, whites, grays, and browns, to full-toned colors?
- Take a look in your closet. What kinds of colors do you like to wear?
- Do you prefer simple combinations of a few colors or a full spectrum rainbow of colors?
- Do you prefer an airy, delicate look or one with bold, dramatic flair?
- Mimic the colors found in your favorite outdoor setting. Nature provides a mistake-proof color palette. If you love the beach, try using sea green and blue with accents of sandy browns or whites. If you love the forest, go for deeper shades of moss and clay with soothing brook blue. Be creative.

Color Schemes

Just as when planning the materials used in your kitchen, when choosing color and pattern, think in terms of complete color schemes. A monochromatic color scheme uses many different shades of the same color, which will make a small kitchen open up immediately by allowing the eye to recognize the kitchen as one open mass. A paint chip card will give you a monochromatic range of many different values of one color and can be used as a handy tool when choosing your paint.

An analogous color scheme uses variations of similar colors, such as blues and greens or yellows and pale oranges. Using analogous colors is pleasant to the eye and brings in color and life to a small room. A good way to think about harmonious color is to get inspired by nature. Mother Nature was, perhaps, the best decorator of all, combining a field of yellow goldenrod blooms with soft grass greens and tender young shoots of leaves. You simply have to walk outside to find a peaceful palette that will always work.

Monochromatic Paint colors

- Harbor Fog
- Blue Hydrangea
- Blue Jean

Analagous Paint colors

- Yellow Lotus
- Hibiscus
- Acadia Green

Warm and Cozy

A warm and cozy color and pattern palette will transform a small kitchen into the family center, a place for gathering, a place for lively conversation. This will be a place that will draw people the same way a warm hearth draws people on a cold night.

Warm colors convey togetherness and strength and, thus, are popular choices for kitchens, as well as dining rooms and living rooms. Using a warm, earthy color combination from nature is a good way to bring in colors that naturally work together. A collection of fiesta ware would fit in perfectly with a room such as this.

Reds are bright, bold, aggressive, and full of vitality. Although cooler-shaded reds can tend to be too dramatic, deep shades of red work well to add warmth to kitchens. Oranges have a tendency to overwhelm, so it is best to use a toned-down version rather than pure orange. Pale oranges take on a peachy, delicate effect, while brownish oranges appear earthy and natural. Yellows can also reflect a jarring and disturbing effect when in bright, full-hued tones. A pastel or pale shade of yellow on the other hand can make a small space seem airy, open, and cheerful.

A muddy brown wall is matched with a subtle tan tile backsplash. A window shade in coordinating warm shades of taupe and ruby and an antique copper chandelier make the look homey but sophisticated.

A warm, lemon kitchen creates a sunny small space, while a pale sage ceiling adds a visual lift to the height of the room. Terra-cotta accents complete the earthy feel.

Cool and Light

Cool as a cucumber. Light as a feather. Colors in the cool range will bring a sense of calm, tranquility, and trust into a room while creating the illusion of a larger and more open space. This is an excellent way to create a reserved, elegant sanctuary within the home. This kitchen space is refined, calming, a Zen-like retreat from the worries of the world, a place for rest and careful conversation. Paint cabinets and walls clean white. Accent with cool tile in pale pastels, soothing sea blue, or sage green.

Green is nature's favorite accent color and, thus, works well in all shades with any color scheme already in a home. Green is an excellent way to bring the outdoors in to a dim, windowless space, tricking the eyes into believing the room is larger than it actually may be. Blue is a cool, peaceful color that can be used in every room of the home. Keep the shade of blue you choose in the lighter range to refresh the eyes and the spirit. Darker hues are more sober and work well as accents to warmer colors. Purples and violets are quickly becoming popular accent colors in decorating schemes. Deep purple is a strong royal color that can dominate a smaller space. Keep shades of purple as pale accents throughout a room.

Sophisticated Neutrals

Neutral colors are shades of whites, blacks, and grays. Neutrals are the most popular decorating color because they work well with any decor and pair well with any other color on the color wheel. They can be used in multiple shades and combinations throughout a room for a subtle, sophisticated effect that will not dominate or overwhelm a smaller space.

White is the most open of all colors and neutrals. It provides an excellent foundation for any room. It will make a small room appear brighter, open, and airy. Many shades of white may appear to be the same. A good way to look at variations of white is to place paint shades on a piece of plain white paper to see the true differences.

Black is the most dominating of all colors and neutrals. You will want to use black to accent brighter colors or as shades of pale gray to create a neutral foundation for other pastels.

A neutral palette of white, gray, and black is striking and allows pattern and texture to become the feature of a modern kitchen.

Complementary Colors

A complementary color scheme is the best way to bring in bright colors or to add depth. Complementary colors are shades of opposites used together, such as red and green, blue and orange, or violet and yellow. Each color brings out the vibrancy of the other when paired carefully. It is best to choose one of the two colors to be bolder and accenting it with a paler, more subtle shade of its opposite. Use these to create a bold mood or style that works for your home.

Bright and Colorful

A kitchen can be bright and colorful, adding personality and spice to a decor, but when working with a smaller space, it is important to balance the light and bright in their intensity.

A crisp dandelion yellow pops when paired with a Mediterranean blue accent. A multicolored tiled backsplash adds depth and interest to an otherwise "dead" space. Keeping colors in the same light-dark range will make a room appear larger, tricking the eye with a continuous line of color. Try a trio of pastels, such as sage green, gray blue, and natural beige, or for a brighter retro-look, subtle burnt orange, avocado green, and ochre. Use color that takes from surrounding rooms to create a continuous line from room to room.

Exceptional

For every design rule, there is an exception. As in all design, it is most important that you feel comfortable and confident in your room. Some design plans defy all the rules and succeed. A small room that is painted all black with chrome accents is a sleek and modern approach to traditional kitchen. Floor-to-ceiling red with black accents makes for a striking statement. Nontraditional kitchen colors, such as pink or purple, paired with unusual materials, take on the personality of the homeowner. Have fun and do what feels good to you.

Paint colors

Northern Air

Prescott Green

Montgomery White

A bright pattern of butter yellow and pear green is created by alternating colored cabinet units for an exciting and sunny kitchen space. White walls and pale wood cabinets recede, allowing the colors to take center stage.

Color Response

As we all know, color can work wonders to make a room appear to be larger or smaller. But what may be just as important is the effect color can have on the body and mind. It is important to consider the mind-body connection when incorporating color into your kitchen design.

Red has been shown to raise the blood pressure, heighten a person's senses, and make the body feel warmer, while the color blue has the opposite effect, calming the body and the mind, and bringing a feeling of tranquility and peace.

Blue is an appetite suppressant. It is not recommended to use lighting with a blue tint in a kitchen or dining area, as it will make any food presented appear inedible.

White is seen as a color and, thus, too much can cause eyestrain and headaches. It is always best to temper an all-white space with pops of color to relieve the eye.

Pattern and Texture

Pattern and texture are easy ways to bring in another design element and an added boost of color to a small room. Don't be afraid to use bold patterns or to mix and match to create a graphic statement, but restrict these elements to smaller spaces. Stick with simple or intricate patterns to prevent a small room from becoming too busy. Graphic, simple, or geometrical patterns work well when using many different colors or brighter shades.

Pattern and textures can be brought into a room in many different ways. Try a multi-colored, striped throw rug to bring a bright touch to the floor. Consider wallpapering one focus wall, or if you don't want to invest as much money, buy a selection of art frames and feature blocks of pretty, modern, or traditional wallpaper samples. Frame your view with pattern: add fabric or wood valences to top your windows and hang a crisp pull-down fabric shade. Invest in simple chair cushions or slipcovers in pretty Provençal patterns that accentuate the colors within your kitchen. Place a long table runner in a rich pattern along a bar area or down two sides of a rectangular table instead of featuring individual placemats for a unique look.

Although fabrics should be restricted in kitchens, as they tend to absorb odors and are easily stained, some soft durable fabrics with subtle pattern and texture on windows or on seat cushions can be a good way to bring addition design elements into play. A thick, machine washable throw rug can also soften floors and make chores easier on the feet and back.

The most dirt-resistant fabrics are vinyl, acrylic, polyester, and washable, breathable cotton. Multicolored patterns, such as simple checks or stripes, conceal dirt and dust better than solids. If you decide to use a solid color, stick with earth tones, such as brown, cream, russets, or gray to keep them looking their best. Also keep in mind that the darker the color fabric you use, the more light will be absorbed. In a small room, choose lighter, shinier fabrics to reflect light back into the room.

Subtle soft cotton skirting along a work surface in a washable neutral colored cotton transforms a kitchen from plain to a crisp, vintage feel.

Test Pattern

Using pattern and texture in a small space can be difficult and overwhelming. But pattern and texture lend an added design element that solid paint cannot. Both pattern and texture go a long way to make a room feel more like home. Keep the following tips in mind when considering adding pattern or texture to your small kitchen.

- Be conservative with pattern on a large area, such as on a wall or curtains. Fabric and wallpaper patterns can become dated over time, so if you want the look to last, stick with traditional themes.
- Use a wide variety of prints, such as florals, checks, and stripes, in similar colors to create contrast and interest.
- If you choose a large pattern, such as a bright floral design, feature it in one or two places and contrast it with coordinating smaller patterns, such as a pretty and simple ticking fabric.
- Be sure to bring along paint chips of your wall or cabinet color to help you coordinate when selecting wallpaper or fabrics. It is be a good idea to make sure your wall or cabinet color matches one element of the new wallpaper or fabric to create cohesion throughout the room.
- If you have doubts while selecting fabric or wallpaper, ask for a cutting or sample to bring into your kitchen and live with it for a few days. Tack the sample up at eye level, the same as you would with paint chips, so you can see it clearly alongside your wall or cabinet colors.
- Use larger patterned fabrics on larger areas, such as a long banquette cushion or on a big bay window, to maximize the effect of the design. Smaller patterned fabrics can be used on any surface, from pillows to tablecloths, or alongside a bigger, bolder print to add contrast.
- Airy, open designs with lots of white space can help to open up a room. Try open florals, geometrics, or mural scenes of distant scenes.

The wall mimics an oversaturated argyle pattern. Pair with understated cabinets and cool marble countertops, the combination is pulled back from the edge and makes design sense.

Summary—Creating Your Palette

- Paint trim and walls, as well as opposing walls, the same color to create a continuous, airy feel.

- Ceilings should be painted brighter and lighter colors to allow the eye to travel up.

- Choose a monochromatic color scheme to open up a room and an analogous color scheme to add a boost of life.

- Complementary color schemes also work to add depth and vibrancy to a small space. But be sure to keep one of the two opposing colors a paler shade to keep the room from being overwhelmed.

- Add small hits of color for an exciting, fun, and stimulating space. A colorful backsplash, window treatments, multicolored throw rugs, tablecloths, placemats, and decorative plate settings, dishtowels, and colorful appliances all give a little color boost to the room.

- Cool, pale, understated colors expand a room while warm, dark colors make a room feel more closed in and intimate.

- Don't forget to consider the ceiling color when transforming a small room with paint. Warm, dark colors will make a ceiling appear to be lower, while pastel tints will make a ceiling lift up.

- Limit fabrics to those that are easy to keep clean, as they tend to absorb odors, and are easily stained.

- Stick to simple textures and patterns in fabrics and wallpaper to keep a small kitchen from feeling crowded, but don't be afraid to use some as accents on tabletops, around windows, or on floors for an added design boost.

From the Kitchen of...
Regina Whelan, Benjamin Moore & Co., U.S.

According to Regina Whelan, color marketing manager for Benjamin Moore, a top manufacturer of quality paints and stains, some strategic color and paint choices can change the entire appearance and mood of a room.

A successful color scheme must first take into consideration light, both natural and incandescent, within a room.
"Daylight, fluorescent strips, and incandescent bulbs all affect color. It is important, then, to make a final color selection only after viewing a sample of the color in the room to be painted. This should be done both in daylight, so the effect of natural light on the color is apparent, and in the evening, for the effect of artificial light.

Even the kind of natural light that enters a room throughout the day can affect the way color looks in a room.
"North light is cold and east light is harsh. Rooms facing either of these directions may look their best when warm colors are used, such as the red, orange, yellow, and brown family. Light from the south and west is warm and bright. Rooms facing these directions may need to be cooled down. Cool colors are green, blue, violet, and grayed tones."

Next, it is important to consider the effects of color on space, especially when facing the daunting task of painting a small room, such as a tiny kitchen.
"A small room will appear larger if walls, ceiling, and woodwork are all the same color. A pale, bright color generally works best. Eliminating breaks in the flow of color at the corners and ceiling lines creates the feeling of spaciousness.

A square room can be made interesting by painting one wall a dramatic, contrasting color—usually the wall directly opposite the entrance to the room. Select the color based on the dominant color in the room's furnishings."

Finally, it is important to carefully select which kind of paint to use. Kitchens call for durable paints that are washable and not prone to fingerprints or staining. Varying the gloss level of a paint can also change the feel of a room.
"Flat paint is the most light absorbent while high gloss is the most reflective. Rich depth of color can be obtained by specialty paint techniques, such as glazing, stippling, and sponging. These are also ideal ways to camouflage imperfections on walls and ceilings. A room's details, such as molding or built-in cases, can be 'highlighted' by painting them in a contrasting color in a high gloss."

Collections as Design

To many, the color, design, and scheme of a kitchen are secondary to a specific passion or collection. By definition, a collection is a group of two or more objects. Collections do not have to be costly but can be anything from bottle caps to handmade pottery—any group of items that has meaning to and gives joy to its owner or owners.

Collectors have special needs when it comes to storage and design, but this can become a plus rather than a negative when it comes to decorating a smaller kitchen. The physical appearance of the items that are being collected are already appealing to the eye of the collector. Your collection becomes automatic artwork perfect for displaying and bringing your personality into the kitchen.

Some collections are more suited for display in a kitchen setting, such as glass vases, cake stands, or vintage cookie cutters. Do not be afraid to display any you like in your kitchen, but keep in mind your space and remember that items should be able to be wiped clean in case of accidents or if a buildup of dust occurs. Glass, pottery, silver, wine collections, pot and pan collections can be display as well as taken down and used within the kitchen. Use your collection as conversation pieces, to add color, and most of all to make your kitchen your own.

Custom shelving adjacent to a sunny window showcases a glassware collection. Always stack and store like shapes with like shapes to keep items from looking cluttered.

Keep in mind some special tips to consider when displaying collections. When displaying smaller items on a shelf, be sure to stack items from smallest to largest front to back to get maximum use out of your display shelf. The different sizes and shapes will play off of one another and actually be more appealing to the eye than a grouping of all like objects. If you are hanging dishes or artwork on the wall, you may want to lay a grouping out on the floor to get the right feel. And always have a friend on hand to help you with placement and hanging.

Glass, colored glasses and vases, antique champagne glasses, and found sea glass are popular collector items and all are a beautiful way to bring light and subtle color into a small room. Many collectors set up sturdy shelves in front of kitchen windows to allow light to pass through their collection and cast a glow throughout the room. This also keeps a collection from taking up valuable storage space within cabinets and on counters.

Pastel colored vintage dishes provide a color boost to the corner of a small kitchen when displayed on open horizontal shelving. Place larger or bulky items on upper shelves.

Pottery and decorative dishes can be displayed in the same way that a fine painting or sculpture might be displayed. Bulky pottery items can be displayed at the top of cabinets and illuminated by spotlights to add interest to the upper portion of the room. Colorful vintage or sentimental platters and plates are as easy to display as a photograph after attaching a standard plate hanger. Group together many different sizes and shapes in a standard circular or rectangular pattern for a cohesive look. You may also line plates up as a multicolored mosaic pattern along an exposed wall for an over-the-top display.

Cookie cutters, utensils, antique canned goods, or any other small cooking items are good collectibles to display in small bunches within a working kitchen. Vintage items bring a feeling of nostalgia and interest to a kitchen display. Smaller items can be display on cabinet doors, in a grouping over a hoodless cooktop, or in any open or empty wall space.

A wine collection can make a graphic impression when a floor to ceiling wall rack is installed, although wine enthusiasts recommend you display empty bottles or wines you do not intend to age for a long period of time. Save your best bottles for a wine closet, a wine rack in a cool dark room away from sunlight, a professional-quality refrigerator, or in a special spot in your cellar. For extremely tight quarters, you may want to consider renting a wine locker from your local wine store. You can now find wine stores that feature such storage options for serious collectors for a small monthly rental fee.

Glass shelves with collections of white, transparent, or multicolored glasses and bottles reflect light throughout the room. Try open shelving in front of bright open windows to cast a sunny sparkle throughout your kitchen. Colorful dishes and serving platters can be hung flat against a wall in diagonals, squares, or circles repeats to add color and pattern. Spotlights illuminate the collection and add depth.

Finally, consider hanging very personal and unique artwork that comes straight from the heart. Display a collection of your children's art for a family museum display. Purchase several inexpensive frames and mats and change them out monthly. This keeps your refrigerator clutter-free, protects you child's artwork, and spotlights a new creation every few weeks. It also brings the personality and color of your family right into the heart of the home—the kitchen.

Wine collectors may want to opt for a specialized compact cooling refrigerators to store wine bottles within their kitchen. Newer models can fit into tight spaces under cabinets and out of the way.

Wine Storage Tips for the
Serious Collector

If you are thinking of starting a wine collection or simply want to know the best way to keep unopened and opened wine bottles on hand, keep the following guidelines in mind.

- Wine must be kept in a dark area. Sunlight and incandescent light can affect the aging process and the taste of your wine. Try a hall closet or special cabinet.

- Do not agitate wines. Wines are fragile, especially aging red wines, so store them in an area that is least likely to be disturbed by vibrations and movement.

- All wines should be kept at a consistent temperature. Most wine experts agree that while keeping a fine wine in a dark area is important, an even, cool temperature is even more so. Wines should be stored at a range from 50 degrees to 70 degrees.

- Store wine bottles on their sides to minimize the drying out of the cork. A wine bottle's cork keeps air from entering into the bottle, thus keeping the wine fresh. Storing bottles on their sides keeps the corks in contact with the wine and keeps them moist. It's a good idea to store bottles in an area that is slightly humid as well.

- Store wines in an area where they will not be exposed to strong odors that may permeate the cork, and thus your wine.

- Refrigerate unfinished bottles of wine for no longer than one week. Be sure to bring the wine back to a palatable temperature by leaving the bottle out for thirty minutes before drinking.

- Ask your local wine shop about storage facilities for fine wines that you want to keep longer than a year. Professional facilities will be able to store your fine wine properly when space in your kitchen is at a premium.

Sleek building materials, soaring ceilings, a
canary yellow tower, and a shocking pink wall
create an extraordinary kitchen-dining-living
room in architect Justin De Syllas's London loft.
The statement in this kitchen is bold and modern,
and yet not cold, and continually works to bring
light and beauty from the outdoors in.

From the Kitchen of...
Justin De Syllas, Avanti Architects, London

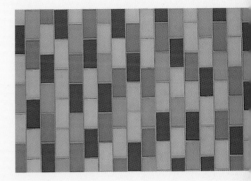

Justin De Syllas achieves an open, sophisticated feel with an emphasis on verticality, color, and function to create a function-oriented combined kitchen and dining room. Here his open kitchen plan encourages family and friends to participate in cooking and working in the space as well as eating and talking and enjoying the end results. In this kitchen, entertaining is as an active, not a passive occurrence.

My kitchen-dining room lies at the heart of my home and is the space through which all others are connected. This arrangement reflects the fact that, for me, eating is a central feature of both family life and entertaining friends. Cooking is carried out in front of guests and although this requires a certain discipline it is found to be both a practical and a sociable arrangement.

The purpose-made kitchen units in lacquered MDF (medium density fiberboard) with white vitrolite glass splashback and stainless steel worktop, handles, sinks, cooktop and hood arranged along one side of the room and are contained at one end by a bright yellow tower containing a fridge and freezer. On turning to follow the stair, the eye is surprised by an intense pink wall.

The whole kitchen was designed to fit the limited space available. The units were made up in MDF and, after being fitted, the doors were removed and spray painted with acid cat lacquer (a tough paint finish which must be applied in a paint booth). By choosing the hinges, sliders, and other furniture fittings we needed from the enormous range marketed by the German company Hafele (a treasure trove), we were able to make the most of every cubic meter of storage space.

Despite its rich and sleek look, a careful eye was kept on the budget, using stock cabinets and materials where possible, proving that good design does not necessarily mean extravagant budgets.

In order to achieve an acceptable level of quality within a low budget, the detailing of all operations was kept simple and robust, with selected factory or workshop components and fittings to complete the basic design.

The refrigerator, freezer, and dishwasher are concealed behind painted doors that match the cupboard units to give a unified effect and the oven and hob are stainless steel to match the worktop and cooker hood. The limited range of materials and the simplicity of the design create a very cool and uncluttered composition in white, silver, and gray, which is contrasted with the bright colors of the pink wall and the yellow tower.

Chapter Four:
Personalizing Your Space

"If the divine creator has taken pains to give us delicious and exquisite things to eat, the least we can do is prepare them well and serve them with ceremony."

– Fernand Point (1897-1955)

You've established a budget, settled on a floor plan, selected your materials and appliances, chosen color and pattern palettes. Now is the time to squeeze in every last bit of storage space, personal touches, and extras into the kitchen. Here are some you may want to try out in your space.

Seating Double Duty

"Wonder well on this point: the pleasant hours of our life are all connected by a more or less tangible link, with some memory of the table."

– Charles Pierre Monselet, French author

Your kitchen will draw your family and friends, and you may want to provide seating for eating, preparation and entertaining. Tables and eating areas allow the chef not only to have more room for prep, but also allow friends and family to participate in cooking and socializing. Kids can do homework while mom or dad prepares dinner. Friends can enjoy a glass of wine and hors d'oeuvres while the main course is finished. Unfortunately, a small kitchen offers little room for tables and chairs, but there are alternatives.

An eat-in kitchen can be created easily. Creating an eat-in can be as simple as providing a designated spot for a glass of juice in the morning, an after-school snack spot, or midnight cookies and milk. When deciding what kind of table and seating you'd like to set up, keep in mind what works for the design of your kitchen floor plan and who and well as how will be using the space, as well as surface material. If you plan on using a table as a chopping area as well as an eating area, make sure the surface material is friendly to double duty.

A super sturdy butcher block table centered within an L-shaped kitchen provides a place for working as well as entertaining.

"From morning till night, sounds drift from the kitchen, most of them familiar and comforting. On days when warmth is the most important need of the human heart, the kitchen is the place you can find it; it dries the wet sock, it cools the hot little brain."

– E. B. White, American writer and humorist

Custom cabinetmakers can include versatile pullout tables for eating or as extra counter space. These tables virtually disappear when not in use, making them the superior choice for the tightest of spaces.

Galley kitchens provide little room for tables or stools. Fortunately many cabinetmakers and furniture stores can create foldout tables that attach to an opposite wall or pull out from underneath cabinets.

Inexpensive butcher block tables offer a great alternative to built-in islands for chopping or eating areas. Be sure to get a stable version with locking casters so that the piece may be moved out of the line of traffic when not in use. This gives the busy chef a place to rest while chopping or prepping as well as a place for family and friends to eat or help out. Kitchen stools can be pulled up from impromptu meals or moved around the kitchen while prepping foods.

Another good alternative in many kitchens is to open up one side to the next room and use a bar setup. This not only opens up the kitchen space to make it appear larger and airy, and gives more room for food preparation, but also gives the person the ability to talk with family and friends while cooking and without crowding up vital floor space. A bar setup will be above normal table height, so be sure to invest in some comfortable and stylish stools for eating and entertaining.

L-shaped and U-shaped kitchens work well with a table set up at one end of the cabinet run. This not only works as a natural place for eating, but also as the perfect resting place for groceries and food prep.

"No one who cooks, cooks alone. Even at her most solitary, a cook in the kitchen is surrounded by generations of cooks past, the advice and menus of cooks present, the wisdom of cookbook writers."

– Laurie Colwin

Finally, you may want to consider a small table setup. A petite table can fit snugly against a wall while cooking and pulled out when the meal is complete for dining. Be sure to keep the table well out of the way of the kitchen work triangle during food prep. A rectangular table generally takes up less space than a round table, but a round table may accommodate more seating when necessary. Whatever table is chosen, it is important to leave a clearance of 2 ½ to 3 feet (0.8 to 0.9 m) all around for chairs and traffic.

Banquettes work nicely as well, providing benches that store nicely under the table when not in use and taking advantage of every inch of space. A corner or window seat setup is a handy place for such seating. Benches work nicely with rectangular tables or across from banquettes and can double as storage when equipped with a hinged top.

This tiny, U-shaped kitchen has a bar set up outside of the work area, opening up the space to adjacent rooms, and allowing the cook to communicate with friends and family while working. A stylish stool is comfortable enough for dining and useful enough for a chef to use while cooking.

Creating a Mood

If you are dreaming of a French provincial kitchen, a sleek modern loft kitchen, or a relaxed country kitchen, you don't have to immerse yourself in endless books of color and wallpaper and building-material samples. Following are some ideas to get you heading in the right direction.

French Provincial

- Warm, honey-colored wood cabinets.
- Sunny, Mediterranean color palette using rich reds, deep blues, and stunning yellows in classic Provençal patterns.
- Nature-inspired patterns, such as leaves, olives and olive branches, and grapes
- Feature chunky, earth-colored crockery and serving pieces throughout the room for display and for use.
- Keep flooring materials simple, such as terra-cotta tile or wood flooring.
- Include a small café table and chairs if there is sufficient room

Classic Country

- Traditional stained-wood cabinets, such as maple, or clean white painted beadboard detailed doors.
- Natural, sunny colors are used throughout the room, especially barn red, dandelion yellow, grass green, or sky blue.
- Basic patterns used on window treatments and as seat cushions, such as checks, gingham, and ticking stripes.
- Skirt farmhouse sinks with cheerful fabrics.
- Use vintage dishtowels as accents on windows.
- Incorporate old armoires or pie safes for storage if enough space is available.
- Decorate with antique or vintage cooking utensils, pots and pans, or pottery.

A family-sized table is added to the end of this kitchen counter. The line of cabinets is seemingly uninterrupted, keeping the kitchen open while providing a place to sit and relax.

Southwestern Spice

- Multicolored laminate cabinets in deep shades or darker woods such as cherry.
- Tile backsplashes in bright, handpainted prints and colors.
- Earthy color, oversized floor tiles or Mexican ceramic tiles.
- Spicy shades on windows and rag throw rugs soften floors.
- Task lighting focuses warm light throughout room.
- Copper or aluminum steel highlights, metallic tile walls, or hanging pot racks add warm sparkle.
- Add a collection of easy-to-care-for cactuses and succulents to a sunny window.
- For a whimsical feel, use tiny string lights and a rustic table and chair set to give a relaxed, outdoor feel.

Modern Sleek

- Use unconventional materials on surfaces.
- Poured concrete countertops are easy to care for and look sleek.
- Stainless steel cabinets, backsplashes, and counters are another way to bounce light throughout a small space and look metropolitan modern.
- Stick with cool color schemes, whites, and neutrals to maintain a sleek look.
- Add bold highlights in oversaturated colors where possible, in floor rugs, art pieces, or simple painted blocks of color on walls.
- Invest in a vintage-modern table and chair set or a tall table and stools for entertaining and eating.
- Include high-tech tools and toys, such as flip-down under-the-cabinet television sets and micro-microwaves, in bold colors for the chef, friends, and family.
- Use sleek high-gloss tile or uniquely shaped oval tile on walls or create a mosaic effect with tiny glass tile.
- Store everything, from pots and pans, glassware, utensils, and pantry items, on industrial racks.
- Light the room with bright halogen lighting.

Whichever style you decide to use, the key is to always follow your instinct. Nothing is off limits as long as it makes you happy. So be creative and enjoy!

An ultramodern, L-shaped kitchen uses sleek and cool materials to create a light, comfortable space. Stainless steel cabinets and workspaces reflect light for adjacent windows. Vistas seen through cabinets are kept free from obstruction, allowing the outside to come in. An appropriate vintage table and chair set completes the look and allows for entertaining and conversation.

"In large states, public education will always be mediocre, for the same reason that in large kitchens the cooking is usually bad."

– Friedrich Wilhelm Nietzsche

Hidden Storage

It is important to hide as much storage as possible to eliminate clutter throughout the kitchen. Cabinets and drawers can be fitted with dividers, slide-out bins, and plate stackers to maximize storage. It is important to avoid stacking things that do not fit within one another to keep dishes, bowls, or cups from becoming bulky or broken.

The backsplash is an excellent area to set up a dishwashing station around the sink. New storage aids provide racks for soaps, sponges, dishwashing liquids, and scrubbers. Keep everything organized in proper containers to minimize clutter.

Try using the space over wall ovens instead of installing a warming drawer. This works remarkably well to warm plates or as a resting place for rising bread dough. This is also a handy place to install a series of dividers or dowels for storage of baking pans and baking equipment.

A two-tiered custom drawer doubles the storage capability of a normal drawer.

Personalized storage is added under a cooktop with special vertical areas for pans, pullout wire racks for pots and pans, and cubby holes for accessories and pot holders. Wicker baskets are handy to stash pantry items such potatoes or onions and fit snugly into bins beneath counter surfaces.

Take advantage of between-shelf and under-cabinet space. Hanging baskets can be filled with silverware or spices. Modular hooks and bars can create an entire work zone for hanging cooking utensils, cups, paper towels, or pot lids. There is now a large range of small appliances that can fit underneath cabinets to free up counter space. Under-cabinet can openers, toaster ovens, even small televisions sets, are now smaller, more efficient, and stylish, as well as fitting up and out of the way. This is also an excellent spot for a mounted knife block or a cookbook holder for hands-free recipe reading.

Be sure to use the back of cabinet doors as well as kitchen doors for storage of awkwardly shaped or large, bulky items. A bin for collecting plastic grocery bags, organizing aluminum foil and plastic wraps, or a roll for paper towels are good ways to hide necessary tools. New racks are specially made to fit on the back of doors to hang tall mops, brooms, dusters, and even ironing boards, keeping items at ready reach within the kitchen but out of the way.

Recess pantry shelves add an extra storage rack to the back of cabinet doors for smaller items such as dried goods and spices.

Necessity Is the Key to Innovation

Redesigning and redecorating a small kitchen can be expensive for the average homeowner. Listed below are some easy-on-the-wallet ideas to help you make changes to your small space.

- Recruiting friends and family to refresh dingy, dark cabinets by painting them with kitchen-safe bright white paint.
- Update scratched wooden floors by sanding and refinishing, or, for a bolder look, painting or stenciling in a design, such as checkerboard or stripes.
- Replace all hardware with newer, sleek shapes and fresh finishes.
- Install cabinet organizers, slide-out bins, stacked baskets, rotating lazy Susans, or shelf boosters, in every cabinet.
- Spring clean all clutter, old pantry and spice items, and transfer all noncooking and kitchen-related items to a hall closet.
- Add a design, such as plaid or simple vines, to wall tiles using special tile paint.
- Sew fresh cushions and slipcovers in simple patterned fabric for chairs, window seats, and banquettes.
- Cover windows with a homemade roman shade and in a shiny polished cotton with a special eye to a trim detail for a simple, yet elegant treatment.
- Paint over or remove dated wallpaper and replace with solid colored walls.
- Replace any faucets and fixtures that do not work or do not meet your needs with newer models.
- Paint an outdated-color refrigerator basic black or white with special refrigerator paint from your local hardware store.
- Install pot and pan racks to add design detail and free up cabinet space.

An island cooktop and counter space is made to look like a farmhouse table, with recessed storage shelves below the surface for cookbooks, decorative crockery, or bulky pots and pans.

Decorating Accents

Mirrors or decorative high-gloss dishes reflect light throughout the room and create the illusion of more space. A grouping of such objects should be lined up and hung at eye level to pull the eye's attention to the middle of the wall and detract from lower ceilings.

Shelves or niches built into the end of a cabinet are good places for extra storage that looks as smart as it is useful. Use small ledges for collectibles or magazine racks for cookbooks or cooking magazines.

While it is important to have fun when decorating your kitchen and adding small details that make the difference from a bland to a polished kitchen, be sure not to add too many small flourishes. Adding pediment tops, filigrees, elaborate moldings, or heavily details to cabinet fronts can quickly become too fussy, harder to keep clean, expensive, and gaudy. Choose one or two special touches to make a small kitchen your own.

Innovation

Using every inch of space for storage in order to eliminate clutter and free up important prep and cooking areas is a must. There are several often-forgotten about spaces that are perfect for hidden storage compartments. The toe-kick area is the perfect space for small items that aren't used often, such as platters and small bowls, a folding step stool or dustpans. This is also the perfect eye-level storage for toys for young children. The addition of a hinge allows the toe-kick to pull down for easy access.

Create a clutter-free kitchen sink by installing a drop-down drawer in the apron. Store sponges, scrubbers, and soap out of sight. Tight spaces between appliances provide excellent storage space for pullout chopping boards. Hang spice racks or utility hooks on the backs of cabinet doors and recess shelves slightly to allow plenty of room for all your accessories.

Paint a panel on the back of the kitchen door with chalkboard paint for an instant and out-of-the-way place for quick notes. Tape off a square or rectangle in any size, trim with store-bought trim and paint the center for a "wall-mounted" message center. Give children and adults, a place to express their creative side by painting the wall from a chair rail to the floor with the same chalkboard paint. Take a good look at your kitchen and make it your own. Be innovative!

Trailer Kitsch Kitchens

What could be smaller than a kitchen found in a tiny vintage trailer? These tiny treasures were built specifically to be efficient, durable, and hard-working as well as being stylish, giving new meaning to the term roadside dining: Meals on wheels?

Trailer-home owners Wayne and Kathy Ferguson have extensive experience in rebuilding and renovating vintage trailers. They have a 1958 Arrowhead trailer they rescued. They offer advice on how to find, restore, and enjoy a vintage trailer of your own.

How does one go about finding a vintage trailer and, more importantly, restoring one?

Finding a vintage trailer is getting both easier and harder! As the popularity of vintage trailers grows, it is easier to find them for sale in conventional vehicle publications, the Internet, trailer club Web sites, etc. It is also harder to find that bargain trailer sitting out on the curb or in a lot waiting for a buyer. We have learned to keep a sharp eye out while traveling. Look behind fences, garages, sheds and barns as you drive. Watch for blue tarps. They may be covering a traveling treasure!

Research is the key to an authentic restoration, but accurate documentation on many trailers is difficult to find. This is especially true for the average "bread box" trailer. Most moderately priced trailers had a life expectancy of only ten to fifteen years. They were "disposable" luxury items never intended to be a part of the next decade, let alone the next century! With scores of trailer builders coming and going in the business, documentation was not preserved as it is for most vintage automotive vehicles.

Restoring a trailer is often a real labor of love. Room and seam leakage inevitably mean water damage to walls, cabinets, etc. Shiny aluminum dulls, and painted aluminum peels! Restoring a trailer requires both the skills of a vehicle restorer and a furniture restorer, since trailers are basically permanent furniture affixed to the inside of a vehicle.

What design features have you found that translate beautifully to 2002, way beyond their time?

Since every inch of a trailer needs to be useable space, aesthetics had to be combined with function and design. Even inexpensive trailers had decorative features but never at the expense of function. They had to meld the two. A unified look from front to back gives even the most compact trailer the illusion of spaciousness, and subtle changes defined specific function areas.

Are there special storage or design features that translate to an extra small home kitchen space?

Trailers approach kitchen design in terms of function and storage (for example: bench seats with storage inside, corner shelves, overhead cabinets over a dining area, storage built under and over appliances.) Trailers emphasize having a place for everything and everything in its place to eliminate clutter.

Trailers don't skimp on windows. Even small windows over the sink and dining areas add light and a sense of spaciousness.

Keep a unified color scheme but don't be dull! A unique pattern on countertops carried through to a dining surface unifies and expands the space, but can add punch if it contrasts with wall color.

Another great place to have fun with design and color is the floor! Many old trailers had uniform walls and countertop colors but truly splashy linoleum floor coverings!"

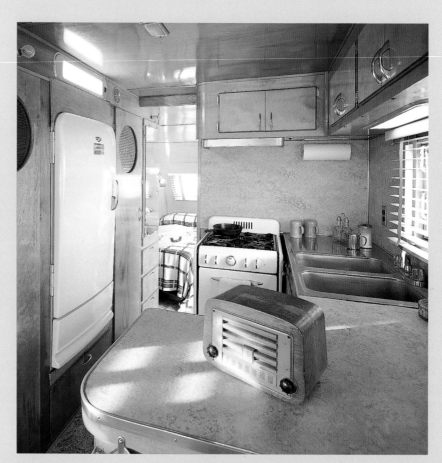

Vintage trailer kitchens are the ultimate in cramped, small spaces. This example makes a tight space feel cozy by using warm lighting, vintage accessories, and brightly colored accents where possible. Trailer kitchens are fun inspiration for any modern small kitchen.

What do you love most about your vintage trailer and, specifically, the kitchen?

It is especially satisfying to know that you have saved a treasured piece of vintage Americana. When we travel and vacation, we inevitably have a knock at the door and meet wonderful people whose memories come flooding back at the sight of our restored trailer. We hear stories of similar trailers and travels: childhood vacations, trips across country, bonfires, and camp songs. We love camping as it was done in 1957: yellow Melmac dishes, Revereware pots, handembroidered curtains, and souvenir pillows on the compact bed!

The kitchen is the heart of the trailer just as it is the heart of the home. The dining table is the center of both recreation and good eating! Games are played, books are read, and postcards are written to those at home. The Princess stove is compact but can bake lasagna and warm bread simultaneously, while the stovetop is used to prepare pudding for dessert and boiling water for washing dishes later. Refilling the block ice for the icebox is a camping ritual done every other day and is far more fun than plugging in a refrigerator!

What do we love about our vintage trailer and its kitchen? Everything!

Summary

- Creating a seating area within a small kitchen is easier than one might think. In its simplest form, you merely need one clutter-free zone, away from small appliances and work areas, for a quick bowl of cereal or a midnight snack.

- Pullout or foldout tables attached to walls or within cabinets work best for a galley kitchen, and are a fun alternative in any other configuration as well.

- Butcher block tables double as prep center as well as dining spot. Persuade friends to help out with the cooking and chopping while enjoying a glass of wine and hors d'oeuvres.

- Another good option is the bar setup that opens a kitchen to adjacent rooms to allow a cook to converse with family and friends while working or entertaining.

- Keep in mind, a small table requires at least $2^1/_2$ feet to 3 feet of (0.8 m to 0.9 m) clearance all around for chairs and traffic.

- A rectangular table will take up less space in a small kitchen, while a round table can be more flexible when adding more seating.

- Banquettes and benches are seating space savers; they can fit against walls and windows and can open up to double as extra storage in a pinch.

An open loft kitchen looks smart when a modern table is added perpendicular to the galley, creating a T shape. The work island has doors that open on all four sides for extra storage. A hanging utensil rack keeps ladles and spatulas at hand.

Closing

"...gastronomical perfection can be reached in these combinations: one person dining alone, usually upon a couch or a hill side; two people, of no matter what sex or age, dining in a good restaurant; six people... dining in a good home."

– M. F. K. Fisher, 'Alphabet for Gourmets,' 1949

For most homes, the kitchen becomes the true heart of a home. When your kitchen is small, special challenges are created. Spaces are tighter. Clutter can get out of hand. Storage and workspace are limited. But even with all this in mind, the old saying is true: sometimes the best things do come in small packages. Whether redecorating, reorganizing, or rebuilding you own small kitchen, it is possible to create an organized, effective, and beautiful space that you, your family and friends can enjoy every day. Here are a few final tips to keep in mind:

- Keep things simple. When in doubt about design, decoration, or organization and always remember that simpler is better.
- Eliminate clutter. Recycle, sell, or donate all those items you use less than once a month or create a space outside the kitchen for long-term storage.
- Streamline to your needs. Determine what the specialty of your kitchen will be and focus on creating a space for those needs; skip the extras.
- Provide as many light sources as possible and illuminate every corner.
- Decorate in a manner that makes you happy. You are going to be living with your kitchen every day, so use colors and materials that make you feel good.
- Most importantly, be creative, and have fun.

Glossary

Analogous color scheme
An analogous color scheme uses variations of similar colors, such as blues and greens or yellows and pale oranges.

Base cabinet
Base cabinets are those that are installed on the floor rather than onto a wall and are usually deep and tall.

Built-in appliances
Built-in appliances are those appliances that are not freestanding, but have been included into a cabinet box.

Cabinet box
A cabinet box is the main part of the cabinets, composed of its sides, back, and top. A door or drawer is added to create a complete cabinet.

Color hue
A gradation of a particular color. A paint swatch will often have multiple hues of one color.

Color value
The degree or lightness of a color.

Complementary color scheme
A color scheme that features opposite colors on the color wheel, such as blue and orange, yellow and purple, red and green.

Custom cabinets
Custom cabinets are cabinets that are built to a homeowner's custom specs and are handmade by a cabinet craftsman.

Frontage
The front surface of a cabinet.

Galley kitchen
The galley kitchen is composed of two parallel counter surfaces with a center aisle running the length of the kitchen.

GFCI
GFCI is the abbreviation for ground fault circuit interrupter. A GFCI outlet is essential in every room that uses water, as it shuts off automatically when it is exposed to water, eliminating the risk of shock or fire.

Halogen lighting
A halogen bulb is a gas-filled, high-intensity incandescent bulb that projects a warm, neutral white glow to a room.

Incandescent lighting
An incandescent lightbulb is the most common light bulb used in lamps and overhead lighting that projects a warm, yellow glow to a room.

Kitchen work triangle
The area formed between the stove, refrigerator, and sink; the areas in which all the main kitchen activities will occur.

L-shaped kitchen
In an L-shaped kitchen, two work surfaces are arranged perpendicular to one another, comprising the two legs of the "L."

Laminate
A surfacing material, often used for countertops and flooring, comprised of paper and plastic pressed together under heat. Common brand names include Formica and Wilsonart.

Medium density fiberboard
Medium density fiberboard (MDF) is a man-made wood substitute material that is smooth, sturdy and stable and provides an excellent surface to receive pain or decorative laminates or veneers.

Modular
A system composed to separate, individual units for easy construction or flexible arrangement.

Monochromatic color scheme
A monochromatic color scheme uses many shades and values of one color predominately throughout a room.

Soffit
The soffit is the area between the top of the cabinet and the ceiling.

Solid surfacing
Solid surfacing is a sturdy, solid colored material used for countertops or sinks made of polyester or acrylic with pigment added. Common brand names include Corian and Avonite.

Stock cabinets
Stock cabinets are cabinets that are factory made in large quantities in a variety of shapes, colors and sizes.

Toekick
The toekick, or toespace, is the space between the bottom of the base cabinet and the floor.

U-shaped kitchen
A U-shaped kitchen is composed of three counter surfaces that come together to form a "U" shape.

Wall cabinet
The wall cabinet is the upper row of shallow cabinets attached to the wall itself that generally hangs over the counter surface.

Directory of Materials

AB Electrolux
SE-10545
Stockholm, Sweden
www.electrolux.com

Amana
2800 220th Trail
Box 8901
Amana, IA 52205
Tel: 800-843-0304
www.amana.com

American Standard
Box 6820
One Centennial Plaza
Piscataway, NY 08855
Tel: 800-752-6292
www.americanstandard-us.com

Ann Sacks Tile & Stone, Inc.
204 East 58th Street
New York, NY 11231
Tel: 212-463-8400
www.annsacks.com

Aristokraft Cabinetry
Tel: 812-482-2527
www.aristokraft.com

Armstrong World Industries
2500 Columbia Avenue
Lancaster, PA 17603
Tel: 717-397-0611
www.armstrong.com

Bed, Bath and Beyond
650 Liberty Avenue
Union, NJ 07083
Tel: 800-GO-BEYOND
www.bedbathandbeyond.com

Benjamin Moore Paints
Benjamin Moore & Co.
51 Chestnut Ridge Road
Montvale, NJ 07645
Tel: 800-344-0400
www.benjaminmoore.com

Best by Broan
926 West State Street
Hartford, WI 53027
Tel: 800-558-1711
www.bestbybroan.com

Bosch Home Appliances
5551 McFadden Avenue
Huntington Beach, CA 92649
800-921-9622
http://boschappliances.com

bulthaup
84153 Aich
Germany
Tel: +49 8741 80-0
www.bulthaup.com

bulthaup
Los Angeles, CA
Tel: 310-288-3875
www.bulthaup.com

California Closets
1000 Fourth Street
Suite 800
San Rafael, CA 94901
www.calclosets.com

Chicago Faucets
2100 S. Clearwater Drive
Des Plaines, IL 60018-5999
Tel: 800-323-5060 ext. 2
www.chicagofaucets.com

Congoleum
Tel: 800-274-3266
www.congoleum.com

Terrance Conran Ltd.
22 Swhad Thames
London SE1 2YU
England
Tel: 0870 600 1232
www.conran.co.uk

Crate & Barrel
1250 Techny Road
Northbrook, IL 60062
Tel: 800-967-6696
www.crateandbarrel.com

Dean and Deluca
2526 East 36th Street
Wichita, KS 67219
Tel: 800-781-4050
www.deandeluca.com

Delta Faucet
55 East 11th Street
Indianapolis, IN 46280
Tel: 317-848-1812
www.deltafaucet.com

Dupont Corian
Barley Mill Plaza, Building 12
Rts. 141 & 48
Wilmington, DE 19805
Tel: 800-4-CORIAN
www.corian.com

Elkay Manufacturing Co.
2222 Camden Court
Oak Brook, IL 60521
Tel: 630-574-8484
www.elkay.com

Franke Kitchen Systems
Dorfbachstrasse 2
4663 Aarburg
Switzerland
Tel: +41 62 787 31 31
www.franke.com

Frigidaire
Tel: 706-860-4110
www.frigidaire.com

Gaggenau
Eisenwerkstrasse II
76571 Gaggenau
Germany
www.gaggenau.com

GE Appliances
Tel: 800-626-2000
www.ge.com/products/home/
   appliance.htm

Grohe
Hauptstr. 137
P.O. Box 13 61
58653 Hemer
Germany
Tel: +49 (0) 23 72/93-0
www.grohe.com

IKEA
Olof Palmestraat 1
NL-2616 LN Delft
The Netherlands
www.ikea.com

IKEA
496 West Germantown Pike
Plymouth Meeting, PA 19462
Tel: 610-834-0180
www.ikea.com

Jenn-Air
Maytag Customer Service
240 Edwards Street SE
Cleveland, TN 37311
Tel: 800-536-6247
www.jennair.com

KitchenAid
2000 M-63
Mail Drop 4302
Benton Harbor, MI 49022
Tel: 800-253-3977
www.kitchenaid.com

Kohler
444 Highland Drive
Kohler, WI 53044
Tel: 800-4-KOHLER
www.kohler.com

Kraftmaid Cabinetry
Tel: 800-571-1990
www.kraftmaid.com

La Cornue France
BP 9006 95070
Cergy Pontoise
Cedex France
www.lacornue.com

Lightolier
631 Airport Road
Fall River, MA 02720
Tel: 508-679-8131
www.lightolier.com

Louis Poulsen Lighting
3260 Meridian Parkway
Fort Lauderdale, FL 33331
Tel: 954-349-2525
www.louispoulsen.com

Luminaire
8950 NW 33rd Street
Miami, FL 33172
Tel: 305-437-7975
www.luminaire.com

Mannington Wood Floors
Mannington Mills
1327 Lincoln Drive
High Point, NC 27260
Tel: 800-252-4202

Moen
25300 Al Moen Drive
North Olmstead, OH 44070
Tel: 800-553-6636
www.moen.com

Pier 1 Imports
300 Commerce Street
Suite 600
Fort Worth, TX 76102
Tel: 800-447-4371
www.pier1.com

Plain & Fancy Custom
Cabinetry
Oak Street and Route 501
Schaefferstown, PA 17088
Tel: 800-447-9006
www.plainfancycabinetry.com

Rösle
Johann Georg-Feudt-Str. 38
D-87616 Marktoberdorf
Germany
Tel: +49 8342/912-0
www.rosle.com

Directory of Materials continued

SieMatic
August-Siekmann-Strasse 1-5
32584 Löhne
Germany
www.siematic.com

Smeg Appliances
45 Bede Island
Western Boulevard
Leicester LE2 6AU
England
Tel: 0800-952-0711
www.smegappliances.com

Snaidero
Viale Europa Unita, 9
33030 Majano (Vd)
Italy
Tel: +39 0432 9521
www.snaidero.com

Snaidero USA
Los Angeles, CA
www.snaidero-usa.com

Sub-Zero
Box 44130
Madison, WE 53744
Tel: 800-444-7820
www.subzero.com

Task Lighting Corporation
Box 1090
910 East 25th
Kearney, NY 68848
Tel: 800-445-6404
www.tasklighting.com

Thermador Appliances
5551 McFadden Avenue
Huntington Beach, CA 92649
Tel: 800-656-9226
www.thermador.com

Vent-A-Hood Ltd.
1000 N. Greenville
Richardson, TX 75083-0426
Tel: 972-235-5201
www.ventahood.com

Viking Range Corp.
111 Front Street
Greenwood, MS 38930
Tel: 601-455-1200
www.vikingrange.com

Williams-Sonoma
3250 Van Ness Avenue
San Francisco, CA 94109
Tel: 800-840-2591
www.williams-sonoma.com

Wilsonart International
2400 Wilson Place
P.O. Box 6110
Temple, TX 6503-6110
www.wilsonart.com

Wood-Mode Fine Custom
Cabinetry
Tel: 800-635-7500
www.wood-mode.com

Resources

Abramson Teiger Architects
8924 Lindblade Street
Culver City, CA 90232
Tel: 310-838-8998
www.abramsonteiger.com

American Institute of Architects (AIA)
1735 New York Avenue, NW
Washington, DC 20006
Tel: 800-242-3837
www.aia.org

American Society of Interior Designers (ASID)
608 Massachusetts Avenue, N.E.
Washington, DC 20002-6006
Tel: 202-546-3480
www.asid.org

Avanti Architects
1 Torriano Mews
London NW5 2RZ
England
Tel: +44+207+284-1555
Fax: +44+207+284-1616
aa@avantiarchitects.co.uk

Dante's Kitchen
736 Dante Street
New Orleans, LA 70118
Tel: 504-861-3121

Detailed Renovations
400 East 74th Street
New York, NY 10021
Tel: 212-517-8516
Fax: 212-517-8576

Home
20 Cornelia Street
New York, NY
Tel: 212-243-9579

HomePortfolio
288 Walnut Street
Suite 200
Newton, MA 02460
Tel: 617-965-0565
www.homeportfolio.com

Kitchen-Bath.com
www.kitchen-bath.com

National Kitchen and Bath Association
687 Willow Grove Street
Hackettstown, NJ 07840
Tel: 800-843-6522
www.nkba.org

The Right Brothers
McLellan-Perrone Builders
4527 Constance Street
New Orleans, LA 70115
Tel: 504-220-6861

Photography Credits

Courtesy of Jerome Adamstein/bulthaup, 63

Fernando Bengoechea, Franca Speranza, srl, 8

Courtesy of bulthaup, 10; 50; 55; 125

bulthaup/John Ellis, 45; 102; 129; 131

Courtesy of California Closets, 135; 143

www.davidduncanlivingston.com, 6; 33; 85; 99

John Hall, 18; 22; 47; 48; 56; 73; 86; 87; 126

Helmut Hassenrück/Jahres Zeiten Verlag, 15

Rodney Hyett/Elizabeth Whiting & Associates,
    13; 16; 26; 31; 70; 74; 77; 78; 80; 89; 91;
    109

Courtesy of Ikea, 34; 38; 42; 49

Lu Jeffery/Elizabeth Whiting & Associates, 29

©Douglas Keister/www.keisterphoto.com, 121;
    122; 123

Th. Kettnes/Jahreszeiten Verlag, 64

Courtesy of The Kohler Company, 21; 139

Courtesy of La Cornue, 20 (bottom)
John Edward Linden ©2002, 82; 88; 104; 113

B. Miebach/Jahreszeiten Verlag, 93

Marco Moog/Jahreszeiten Verlag, 41

Courtesy of Plain & Fancy Custom Cabinetry,
    62; 65; 108; 114; 115 (bottom); 141

Greg Premru, 58; 106

Eric Roth, 46; 53

Eric Roth/Astrid Vigeland Design, 94

Courtesy of Ann Sacks Tile & Stone, 72; 76; 79;
    92; 96; 105

Courtesy of Smeg, 20 (top)

Courtesy of Snaidero Kitchens + Design, 27; 66;
    67; 84; 101; 119

Brian Vanden Brink, 51; 61; 69; 100

Brian Vanden Brink/Elliott & Elliott Architects,
    36; 115 (top)

Brian Vanden Brink/Winton Scott Architects, 24

Brian Vanden Brink/Jack Silverio, Architect, 25

Brian Vanden Brink/Van Dam & Renner
    Architects, 23

Brian Vanden Brink/Ted Wengren, Architect, 116

Steve Vierra/David Mullen, Architect, 111

Acknowledgments

I would like to thank Betsy, Paula, Wendy, Claire, and Kristy at Rockport Publishers for all their patience, support, and help with this project. Many thanks as well to Benjamin Moore Paints, bulthaup, Plain & Fancy Custom Cabinetry, Abramson Teiger Architects, Avanti Architects, George Monos of Detailed Renovations, Perrone–McLellan Builders, Snaidero Kitchens + Design, Ikea, California Closets, Ann Sacks Tile & Stone, Kohler, Smeg, Sharp, and La Cornue.

Personal thanks to all my family and friends for keeping me writing.

About the Author

Tara McLellan is a freelance writer who lives just off the Mississippi River in New Orleans, Louisiana. She has written for *Metropolitan Home* magazine, *New Orleans Homes and Lifestyles* magazine, and *St. Charles Avenue* magazine. This is the second book Tara has written for Rockport Publishers.